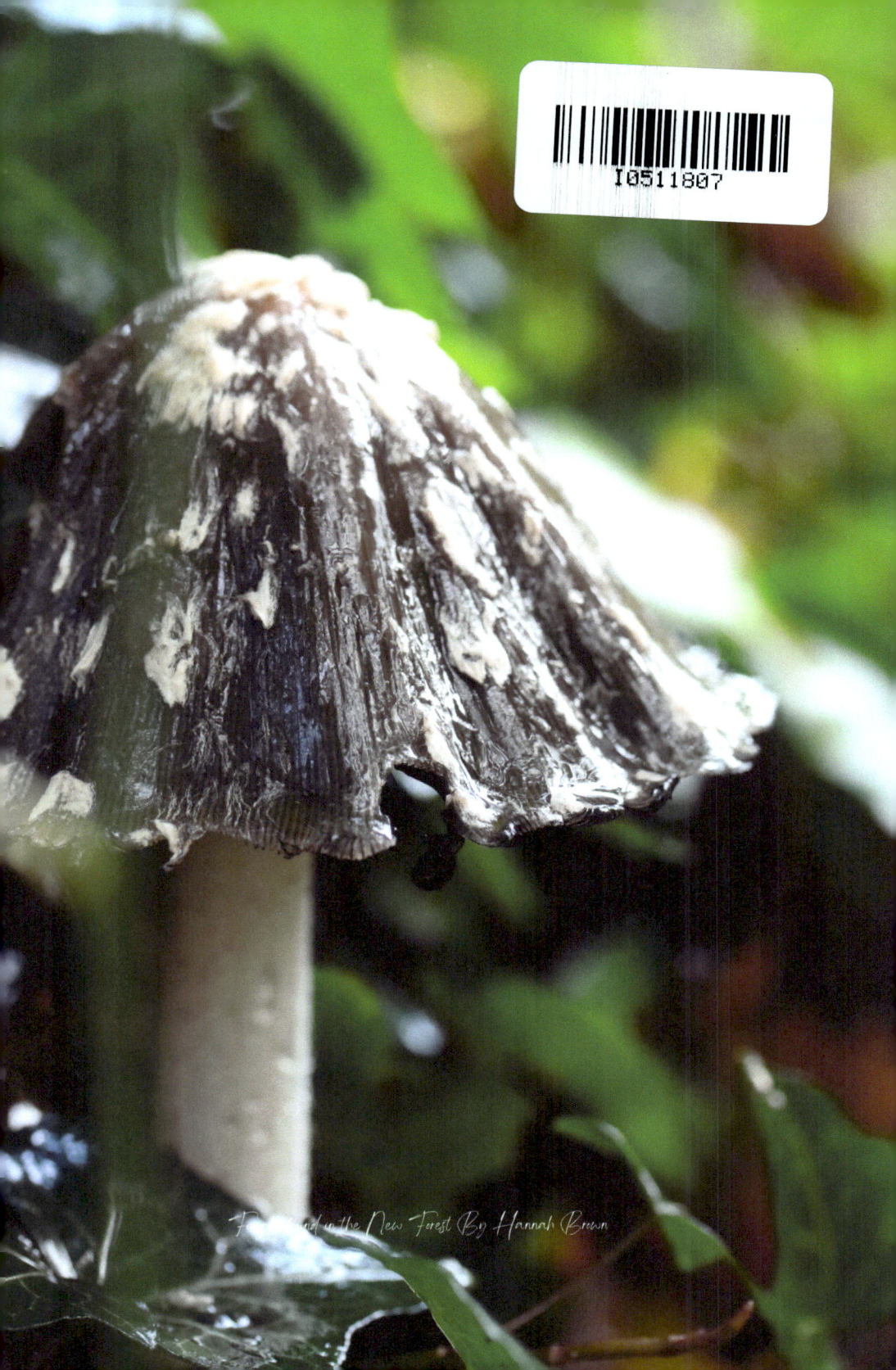

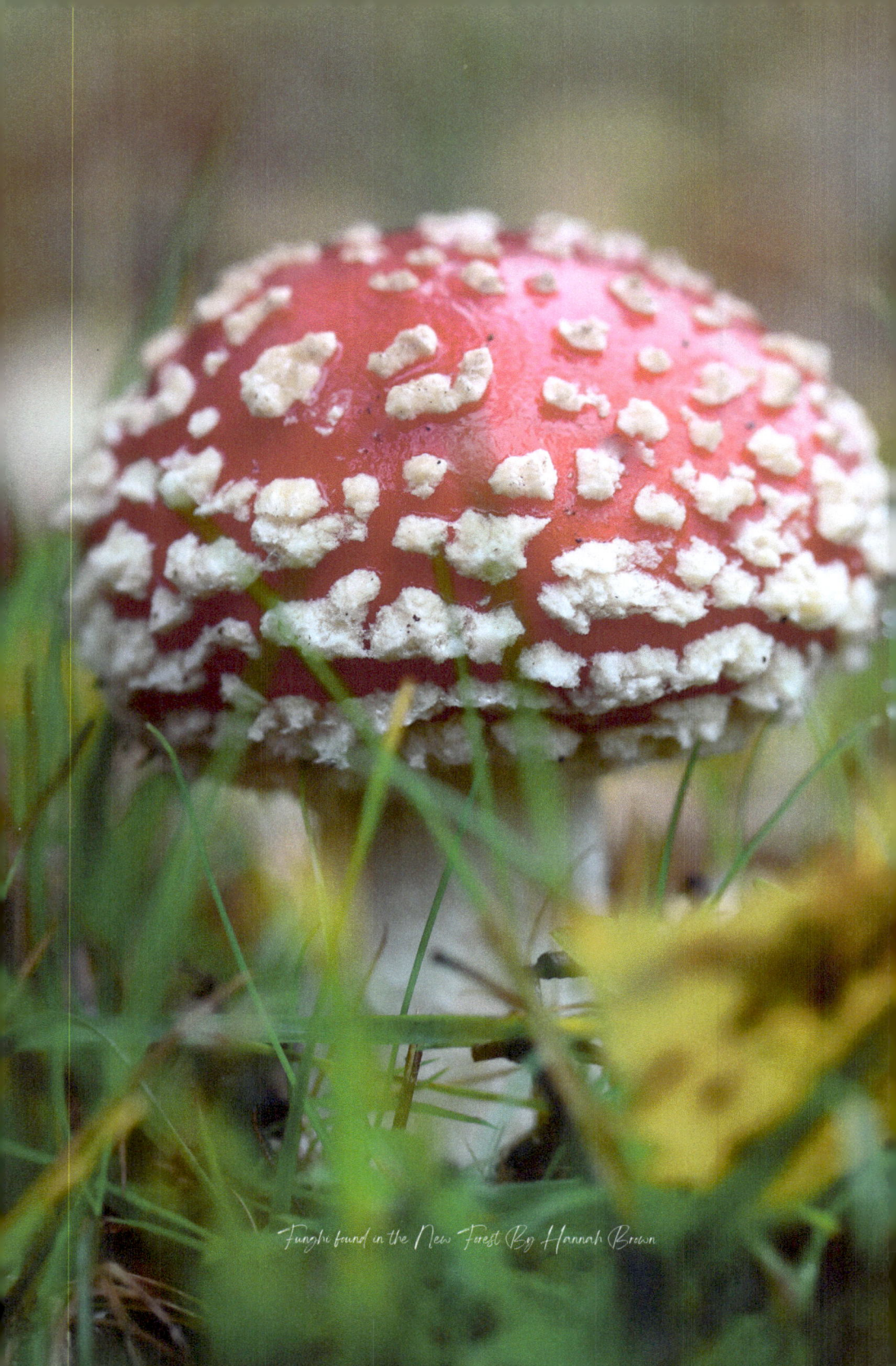

Funghi found in the New Forest By Hannah Brown

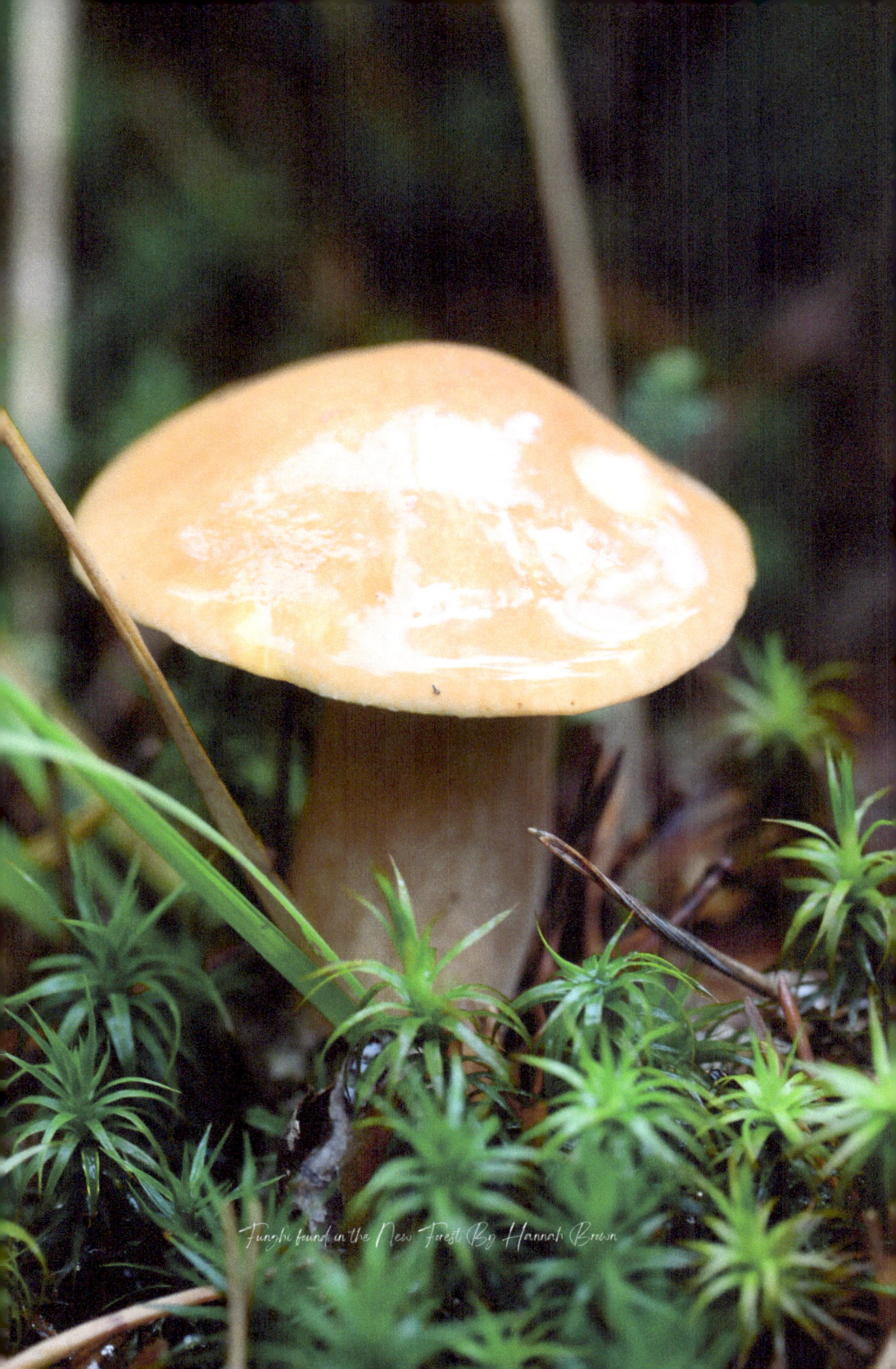

Funghi found in the New Forest By Hannah Brown

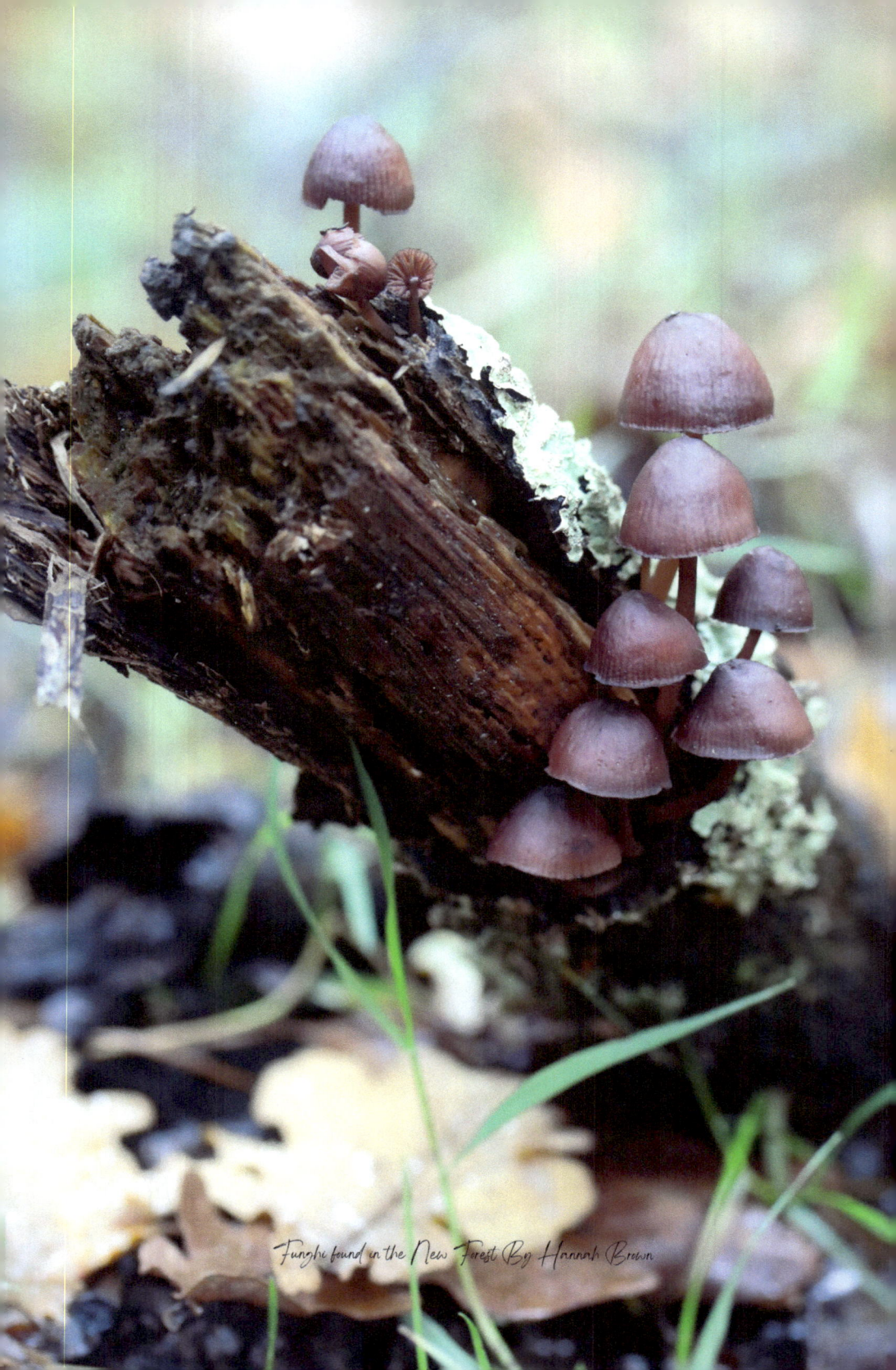

Funghi found in the New Forest By Hannah Brown

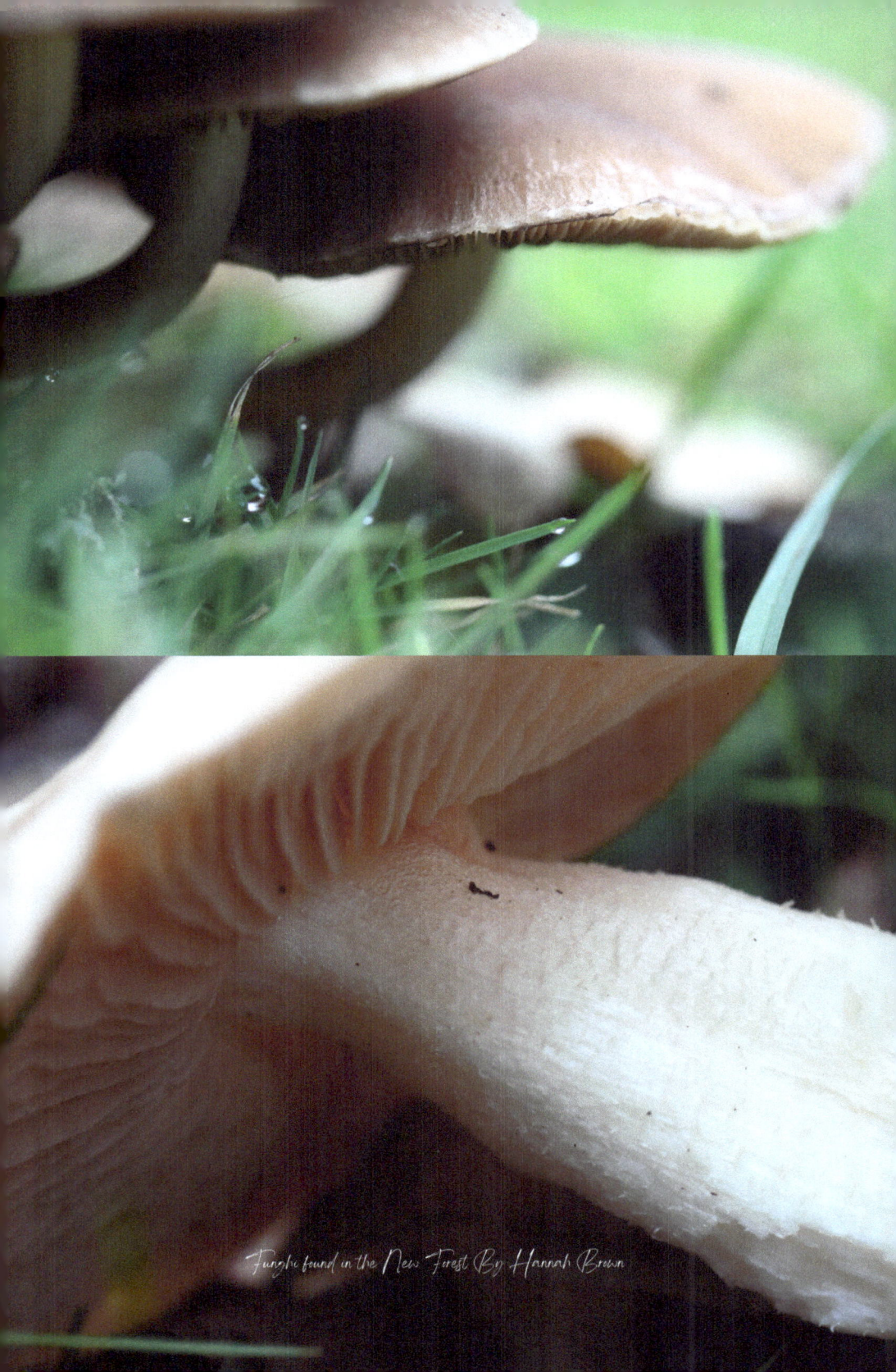

Funghi found in the New Forest By Hannah Brown

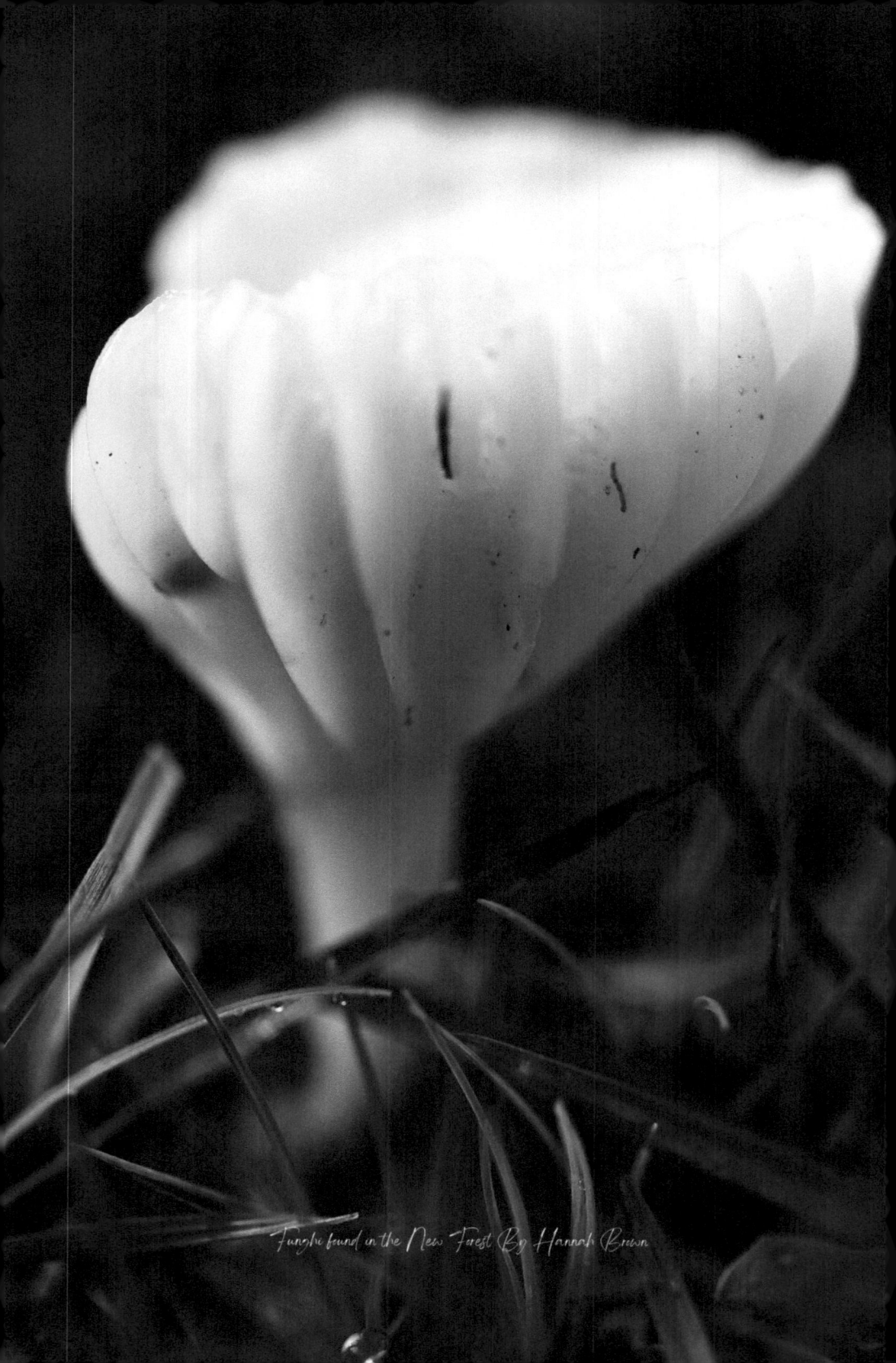

Fungi found in the New Forest By Hannah Brown

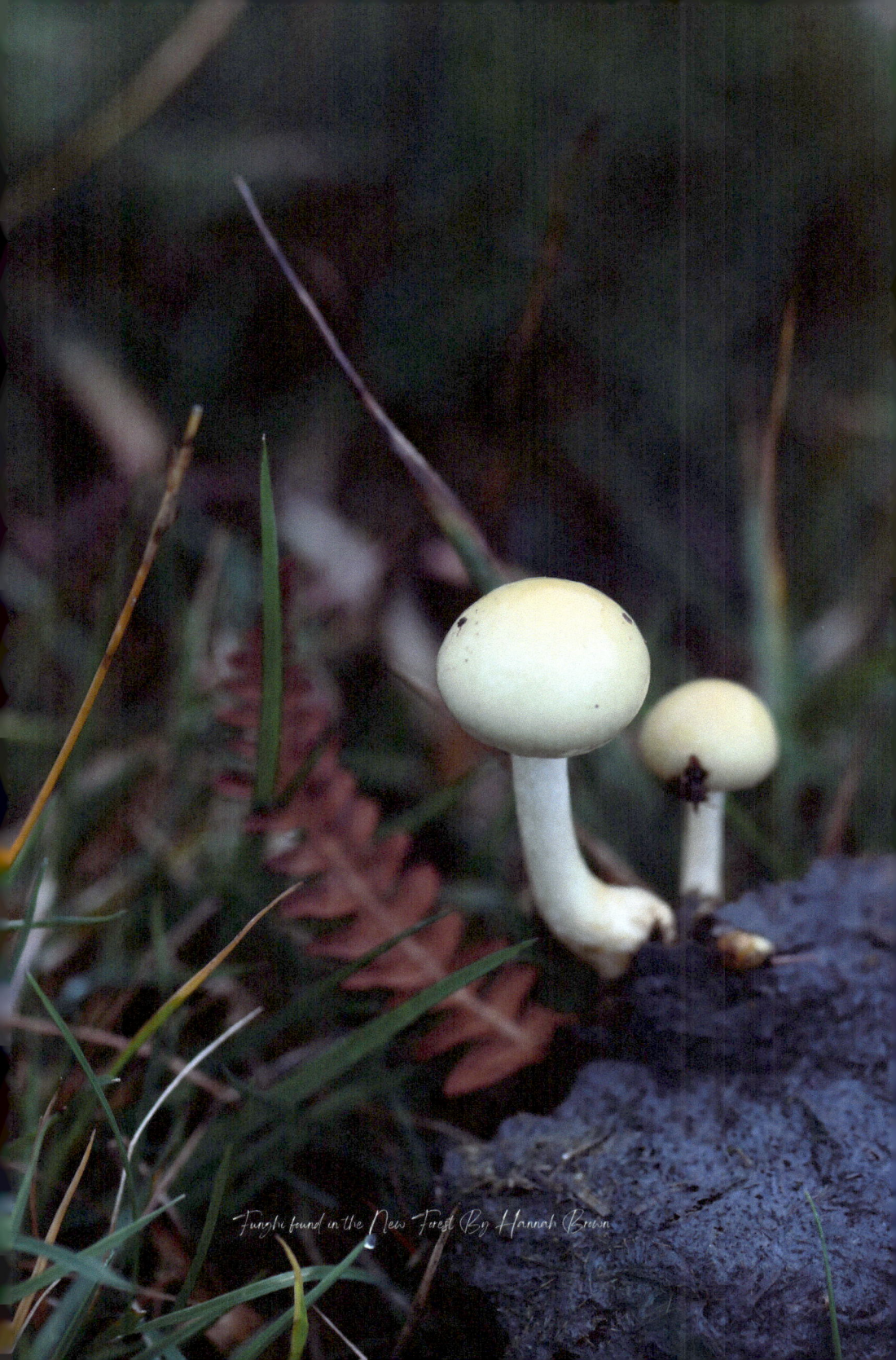
Funghi found in the New Forest By Hannah Brown

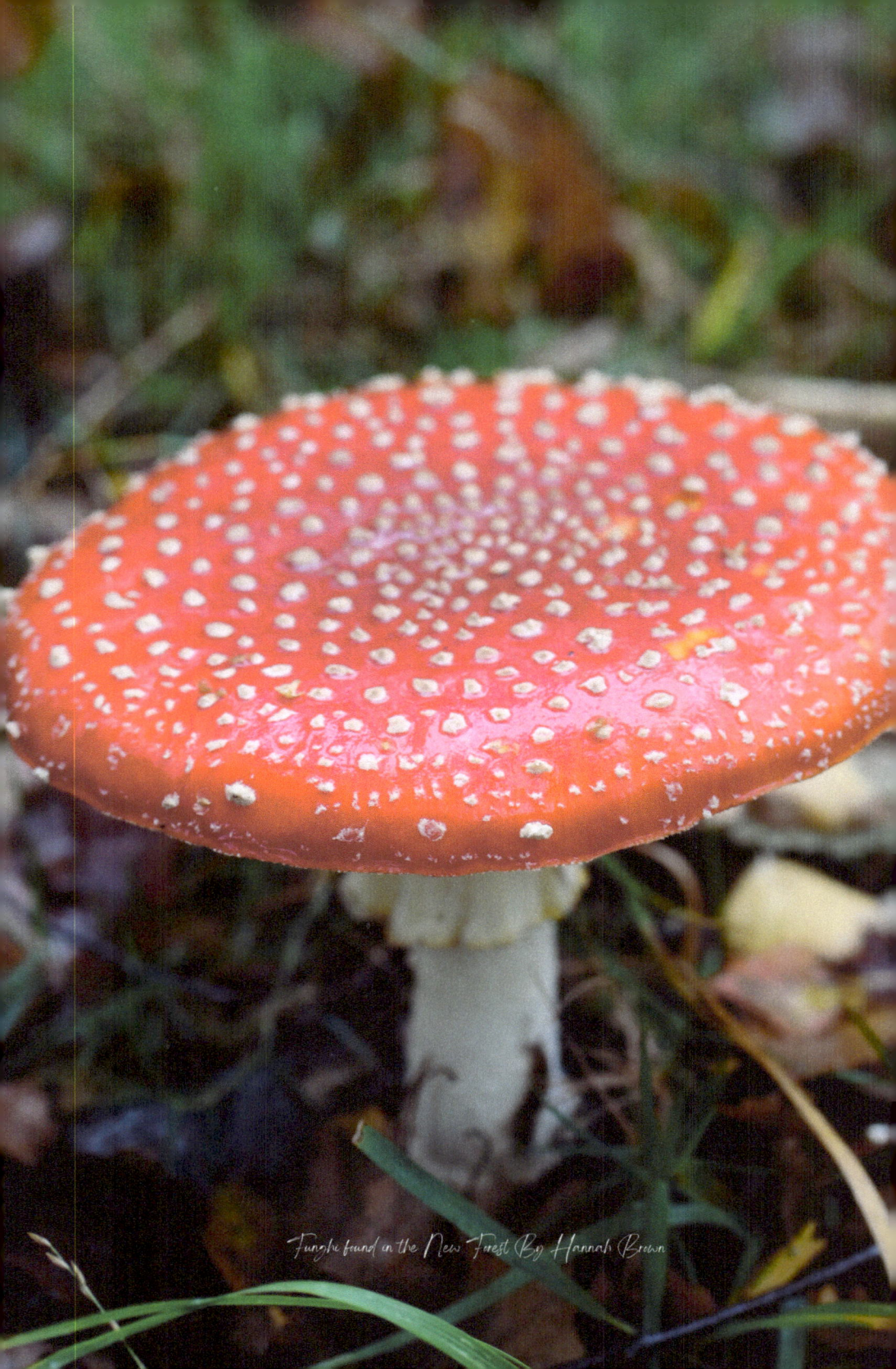

Fungi found in the New Forest By Hannah Brown

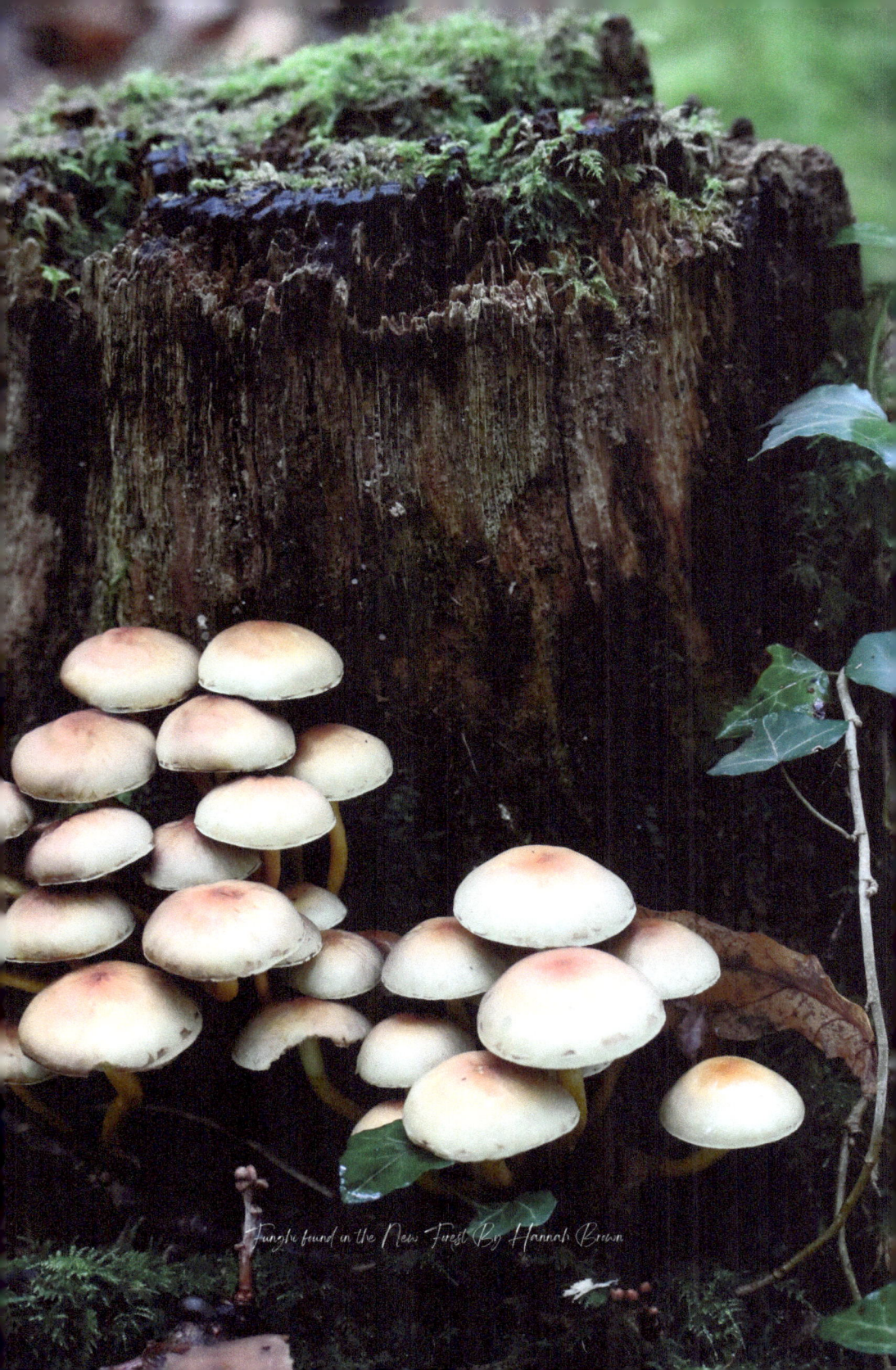
Fungi found in the New Forest By Hannah Brown

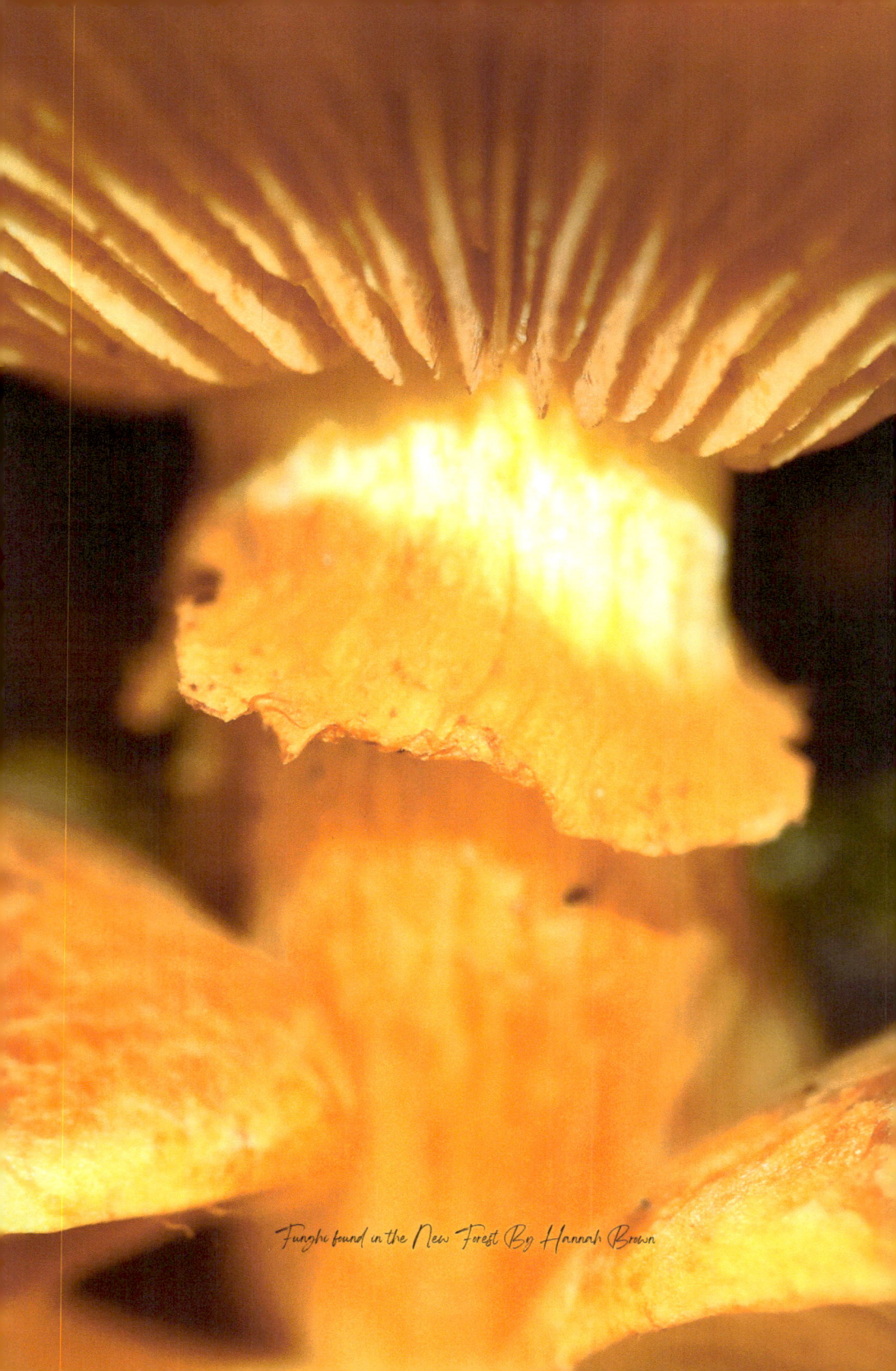

Funghi found in the New Forest By Hannah Brown

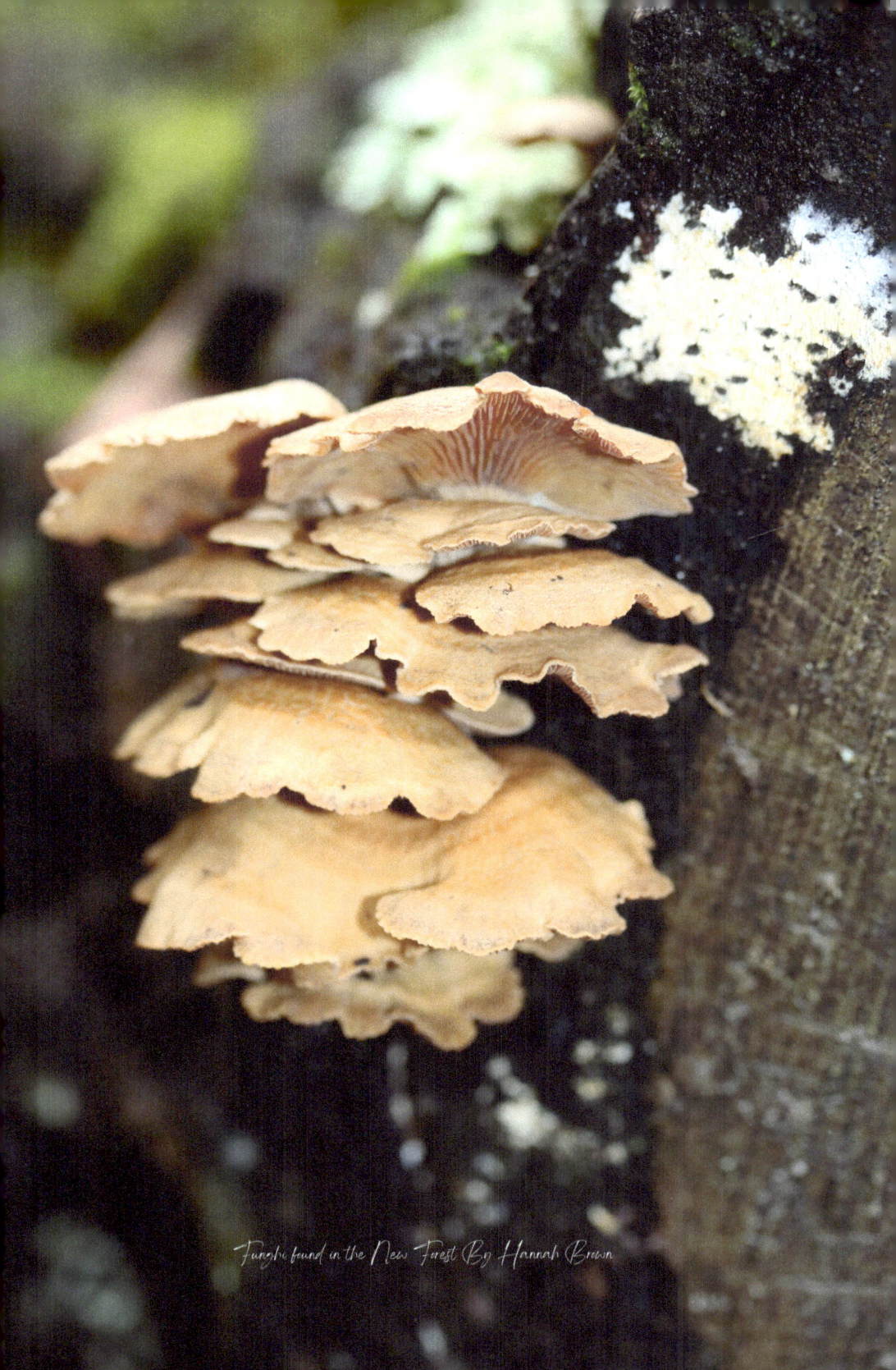

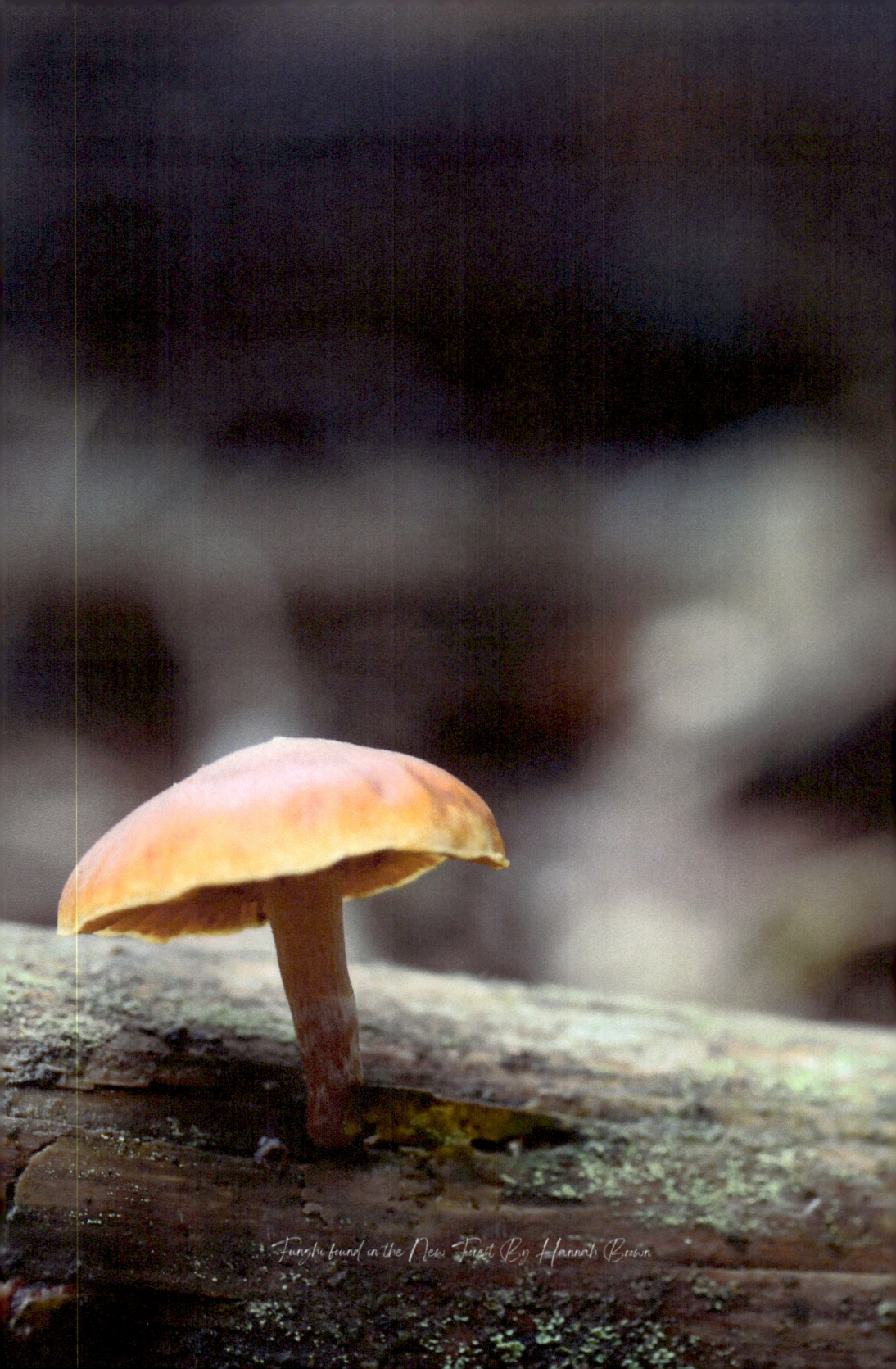

Funghi found in the New Forest By Hannah Brown

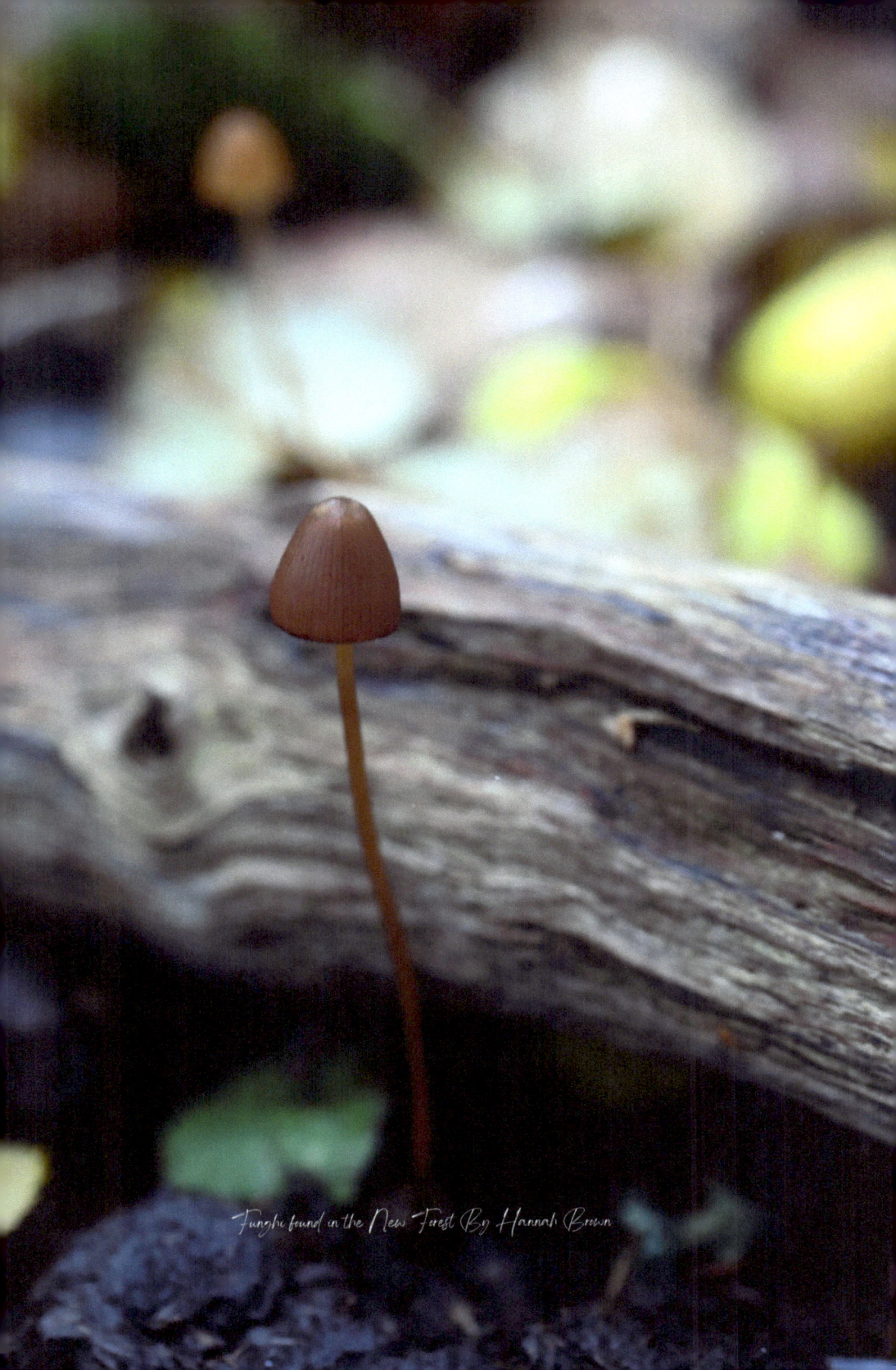

Fungi found in the New Forest By Hannah Brown

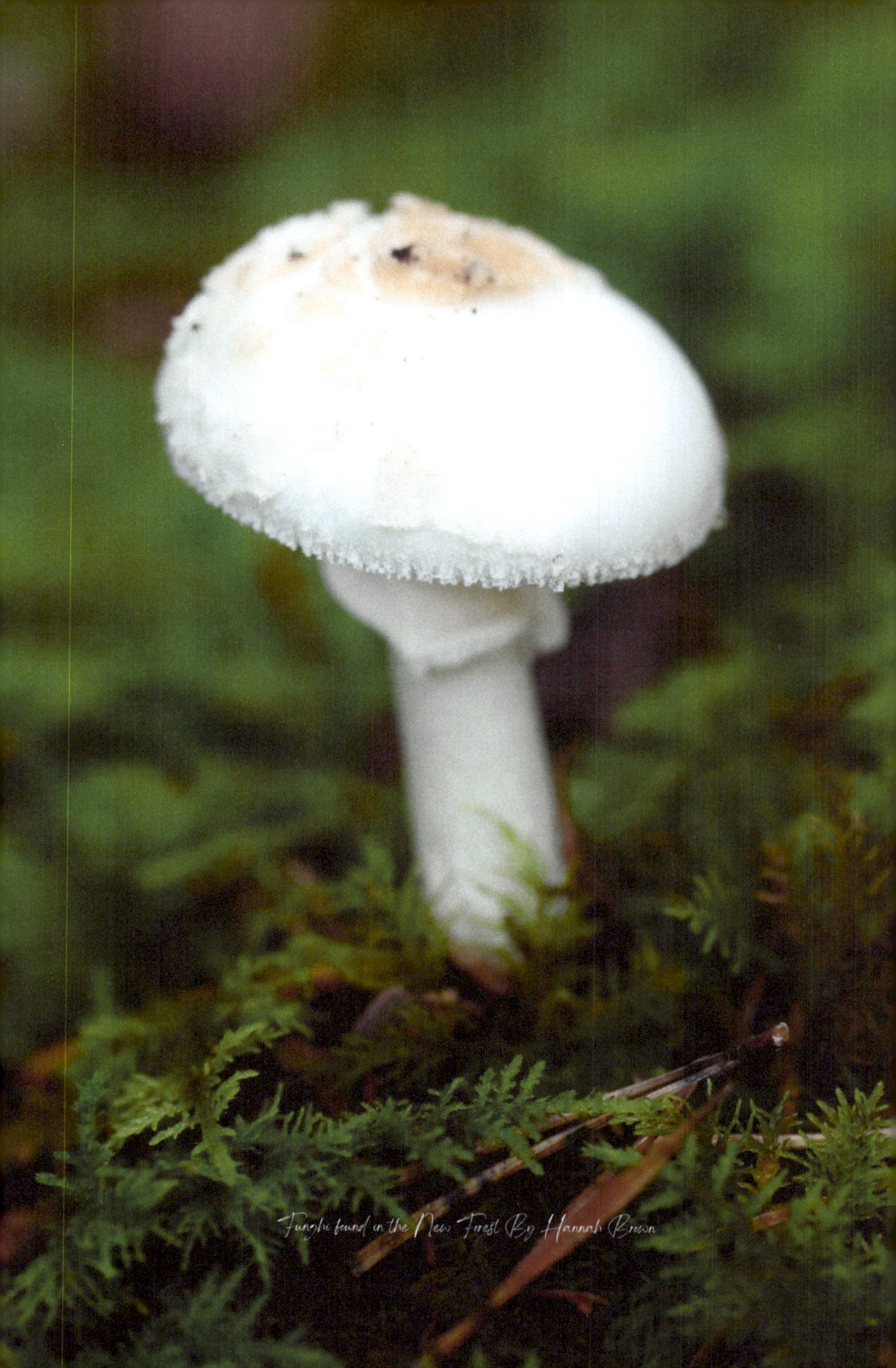

Fungi found in the New Forest By Hannah Brown

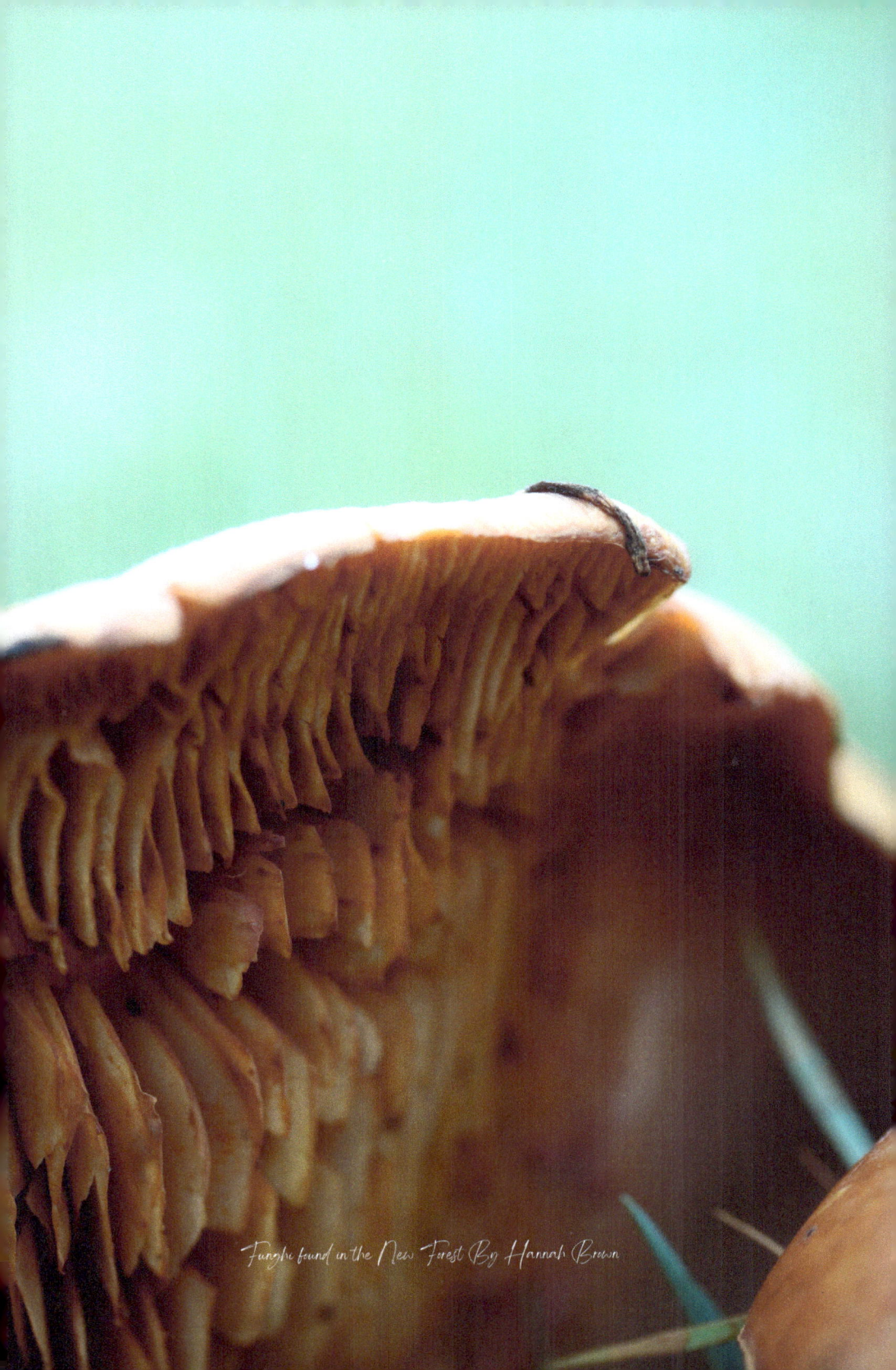

Funghi found in the New Forest By Hannah Brown

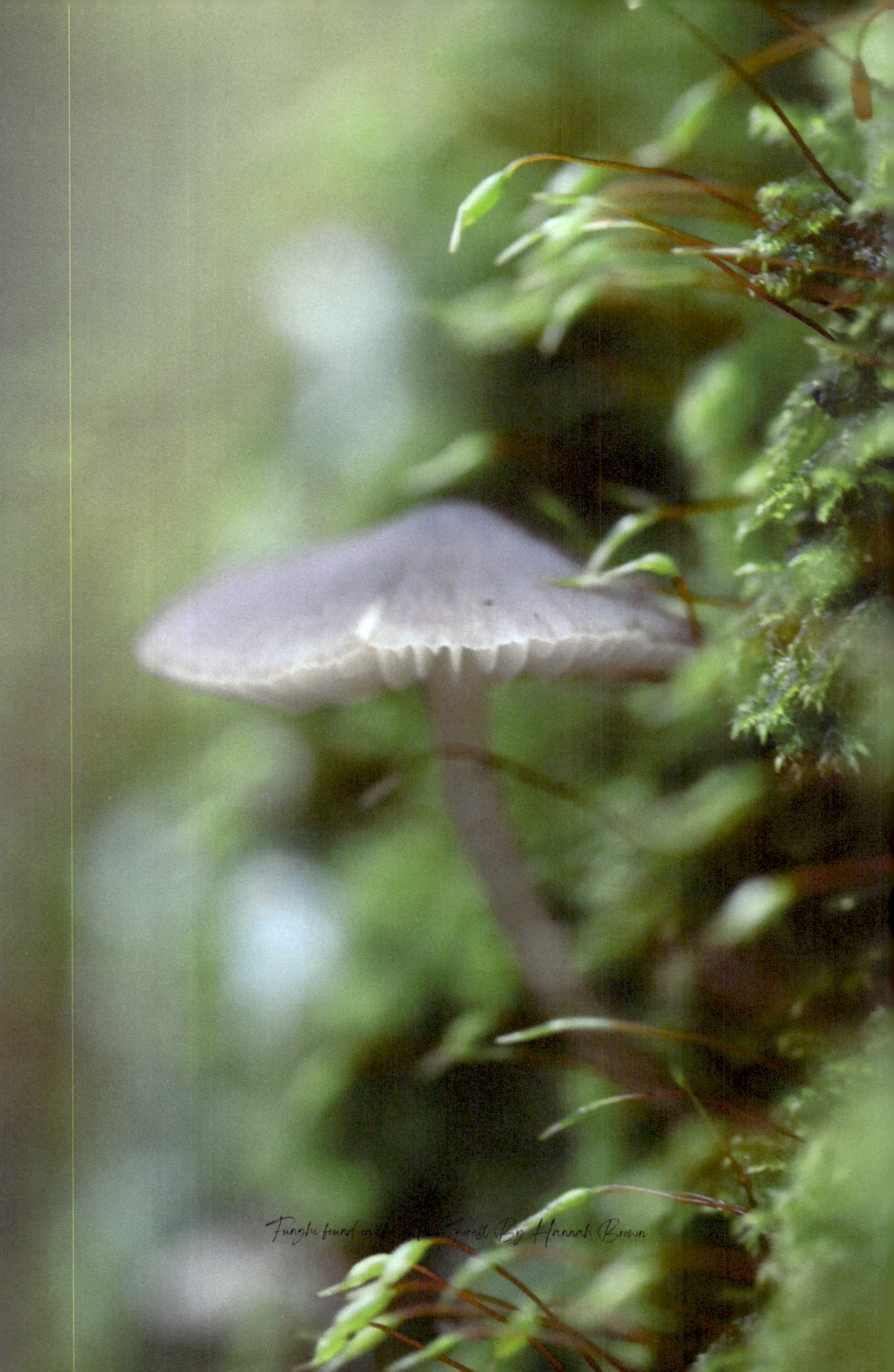

Funghi found in the Forest By Hannah Brown

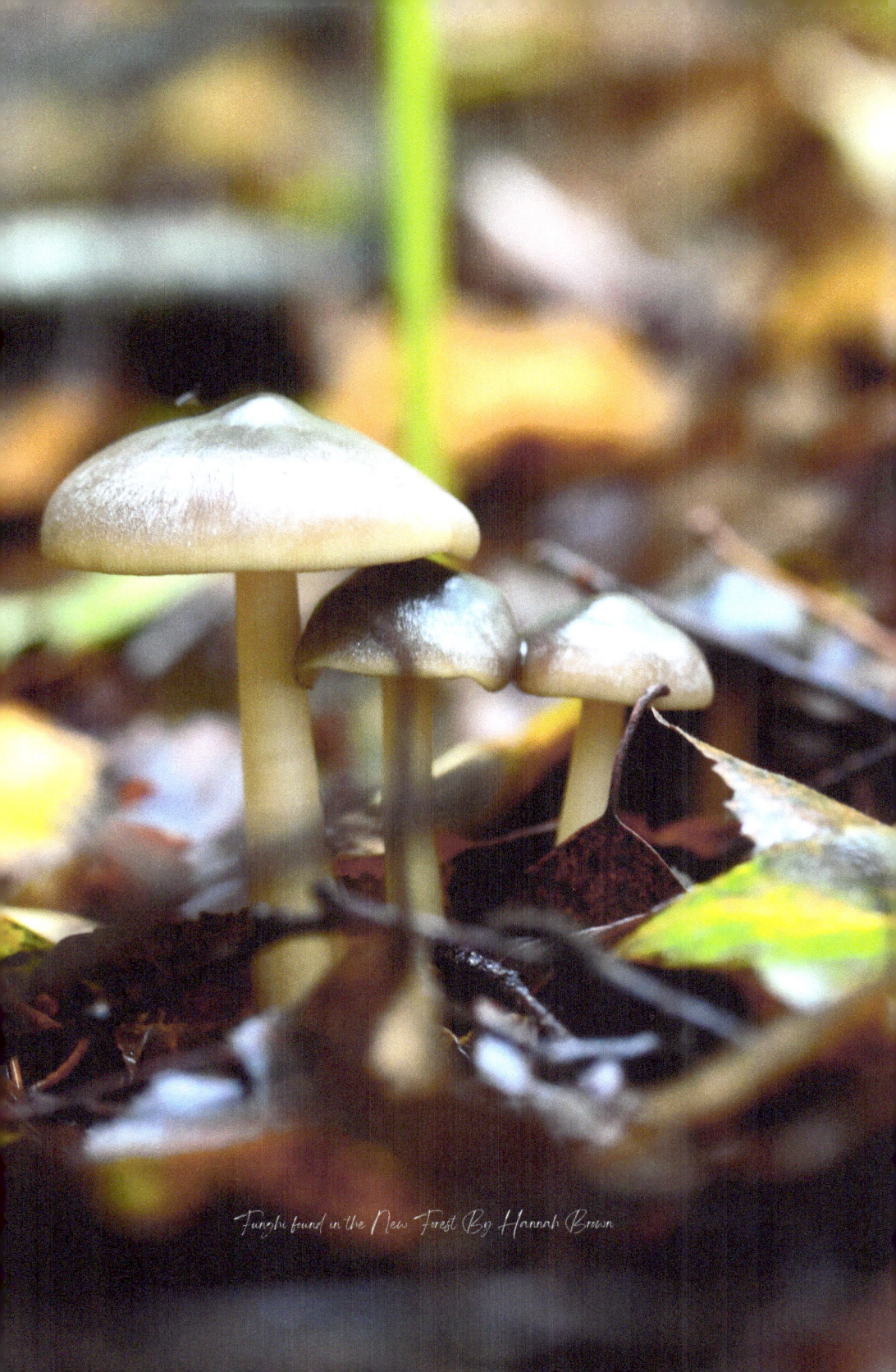

Fungi found in the New Forest By Hannah Brown

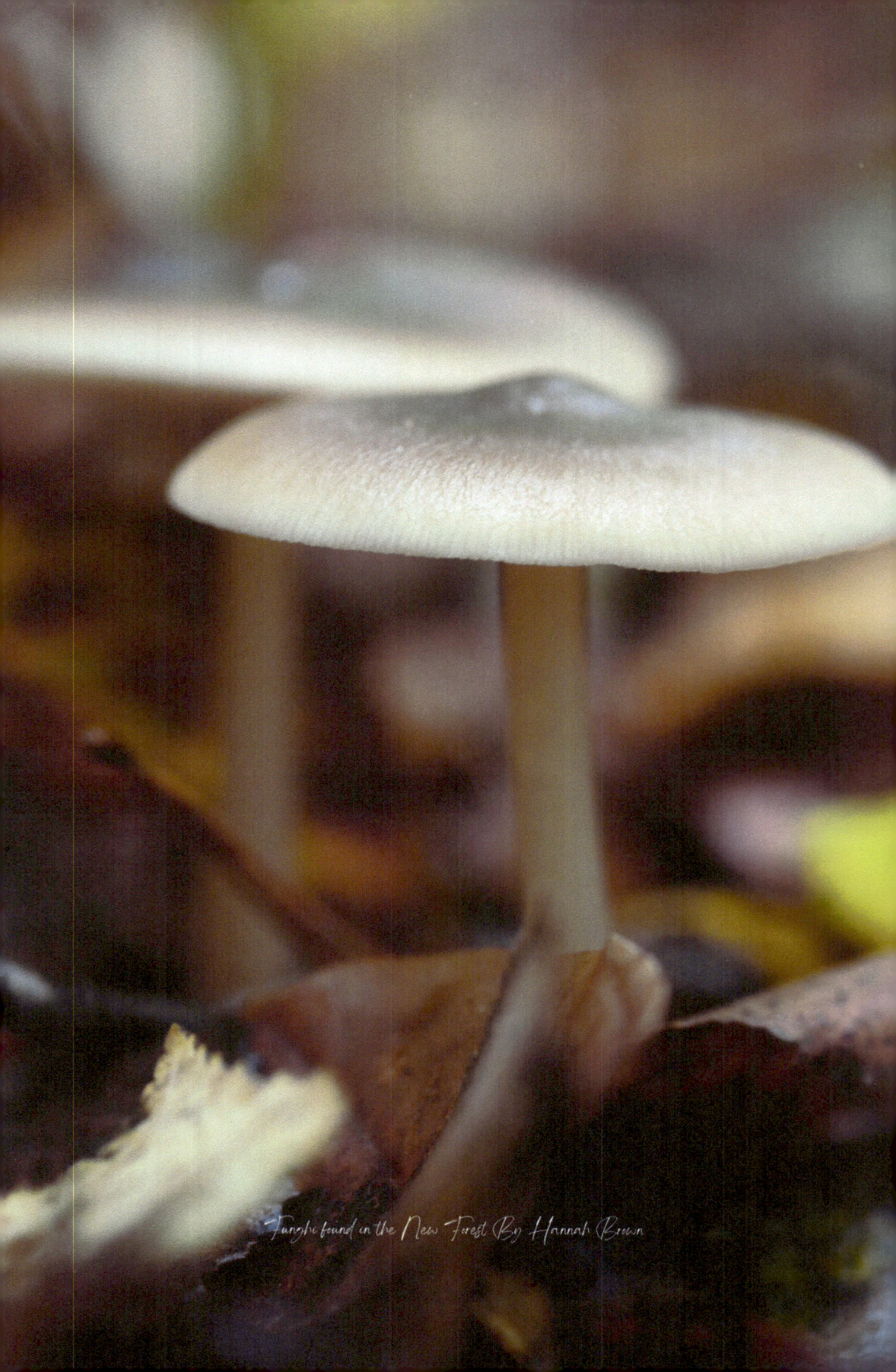

Funghi found in the New Forest By Hannah Brown

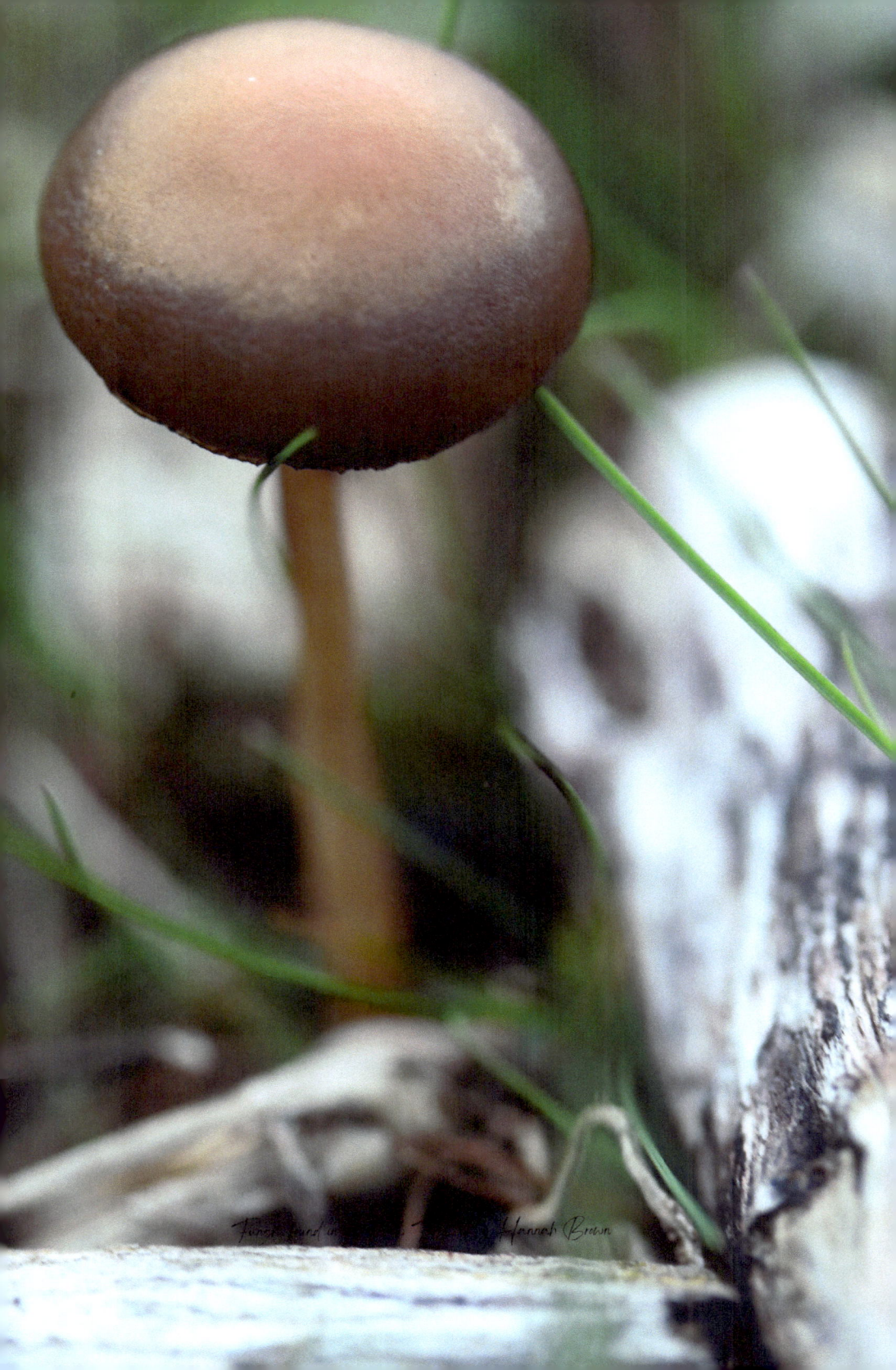

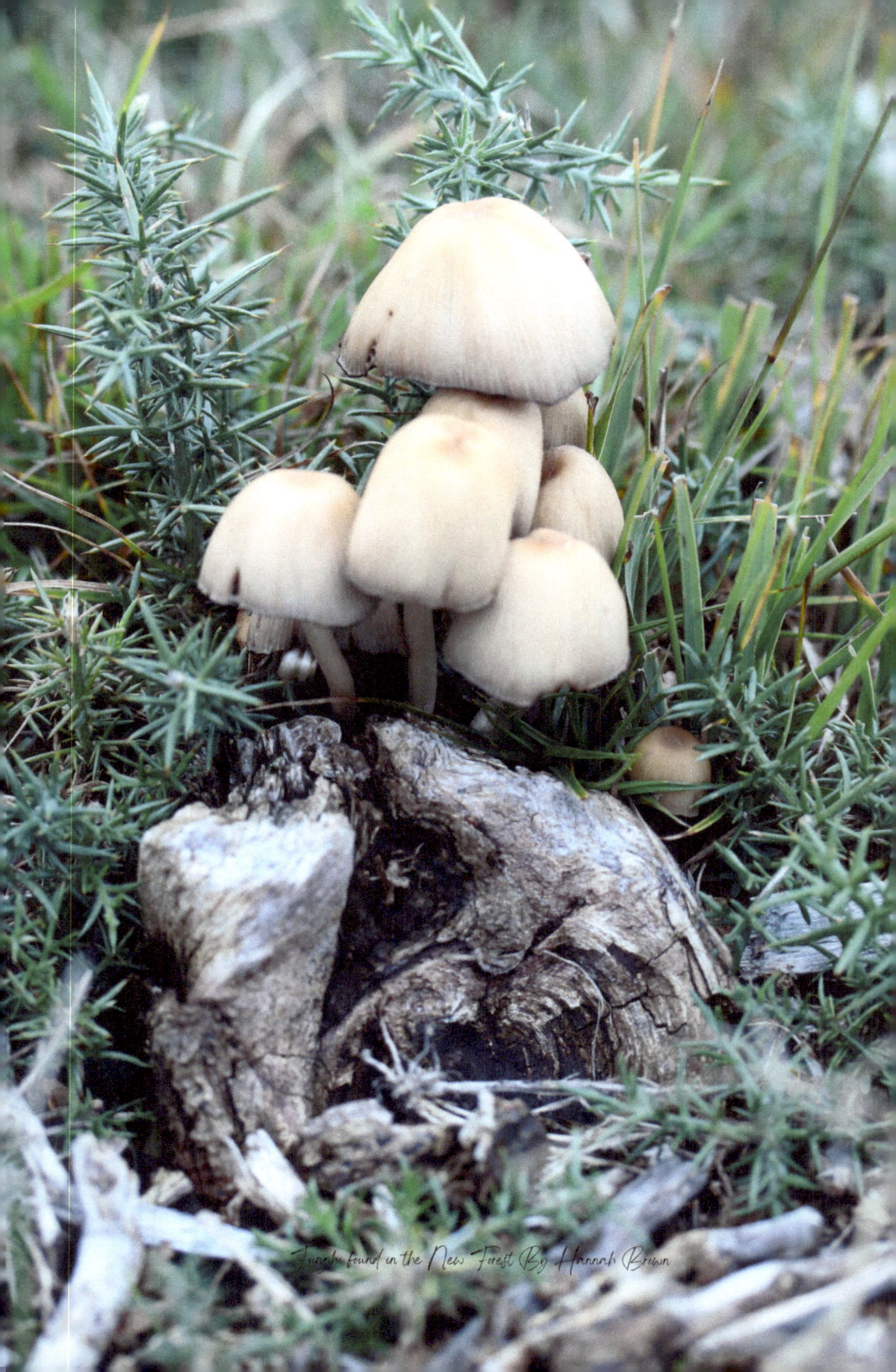

Fungi found in the New Forest By Hannah Brown

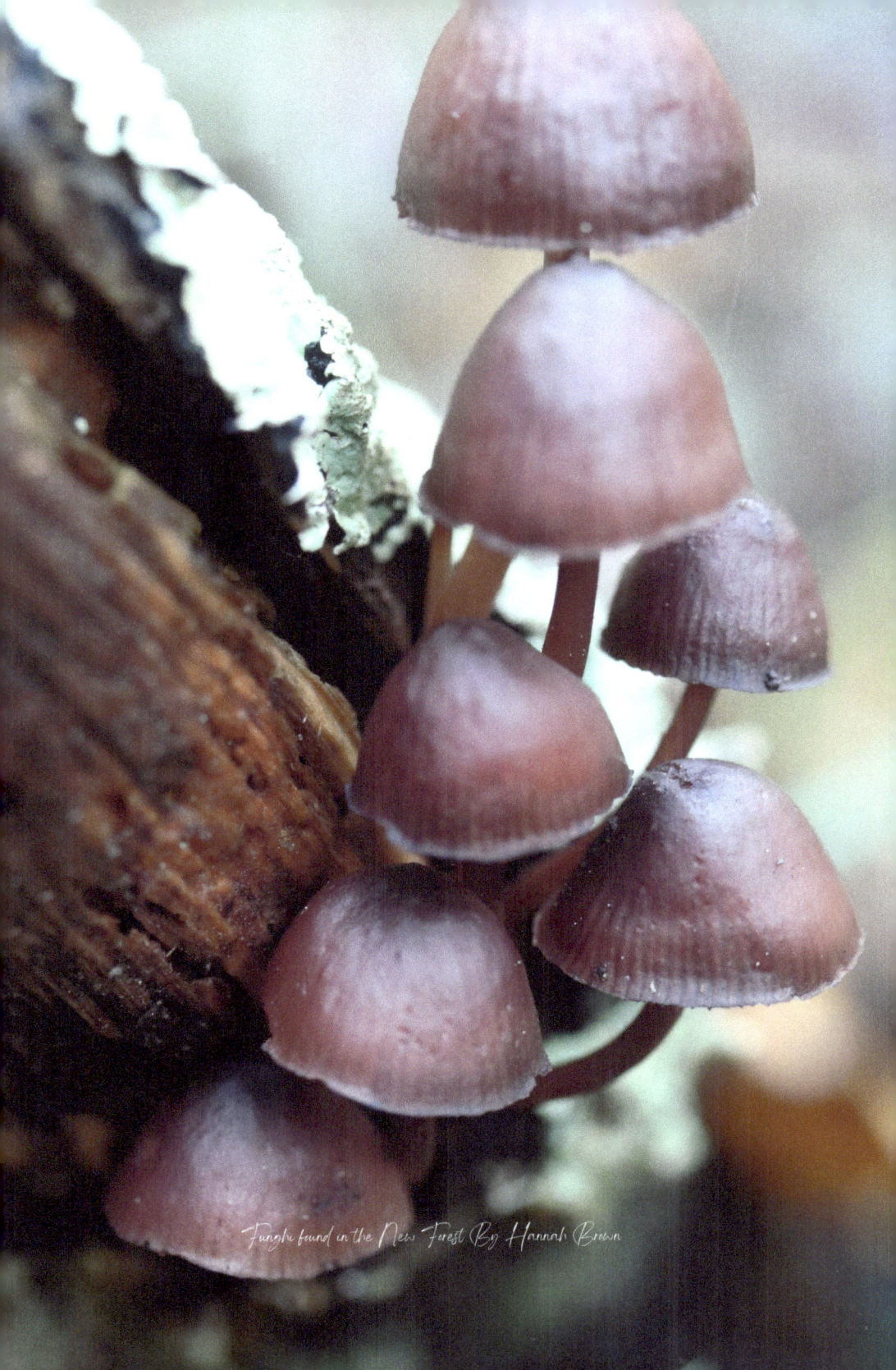

Fungi found in the New Forest By Hannah Brown

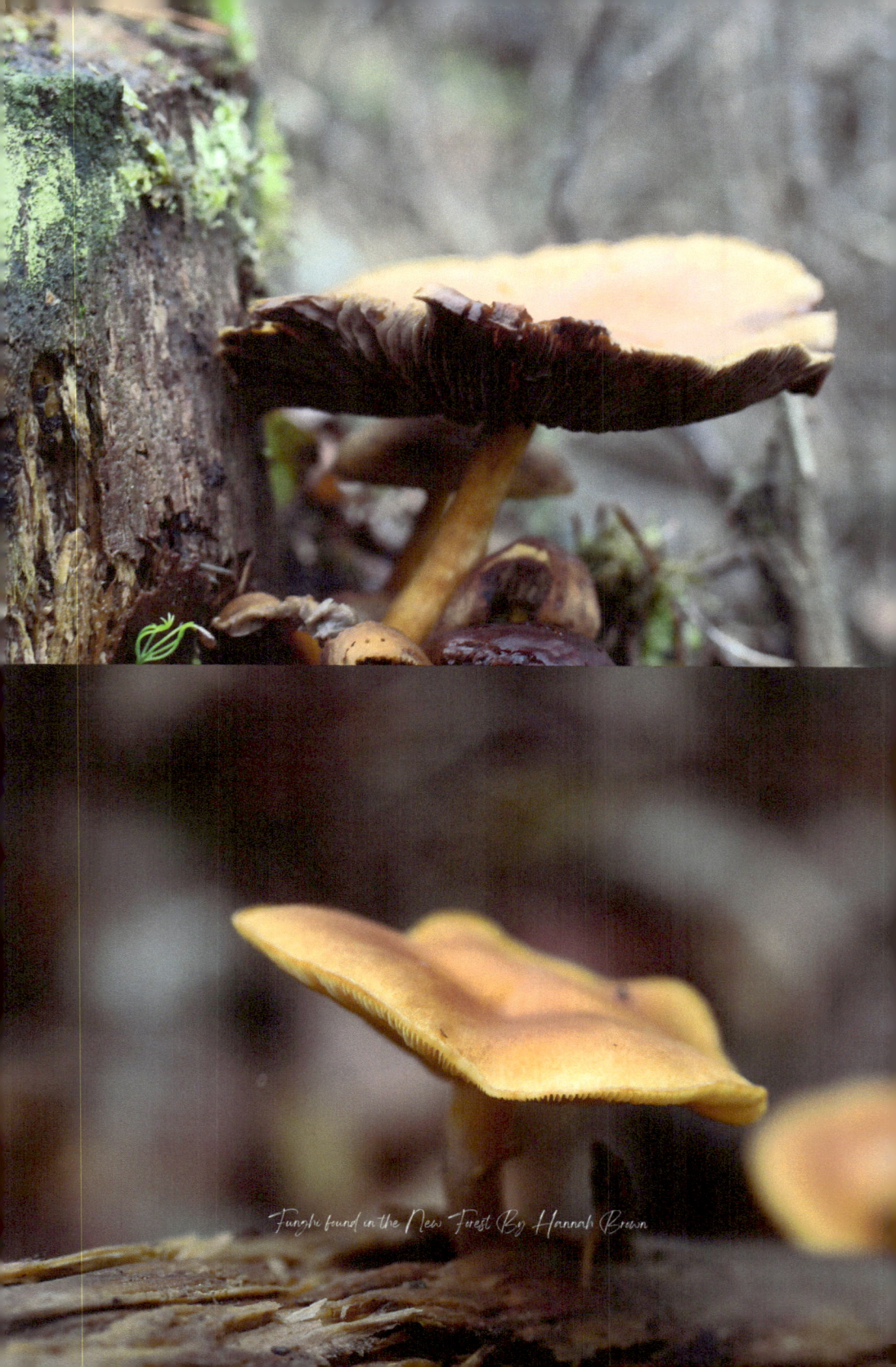

Fungi found in the New Forest By Hannah Brown

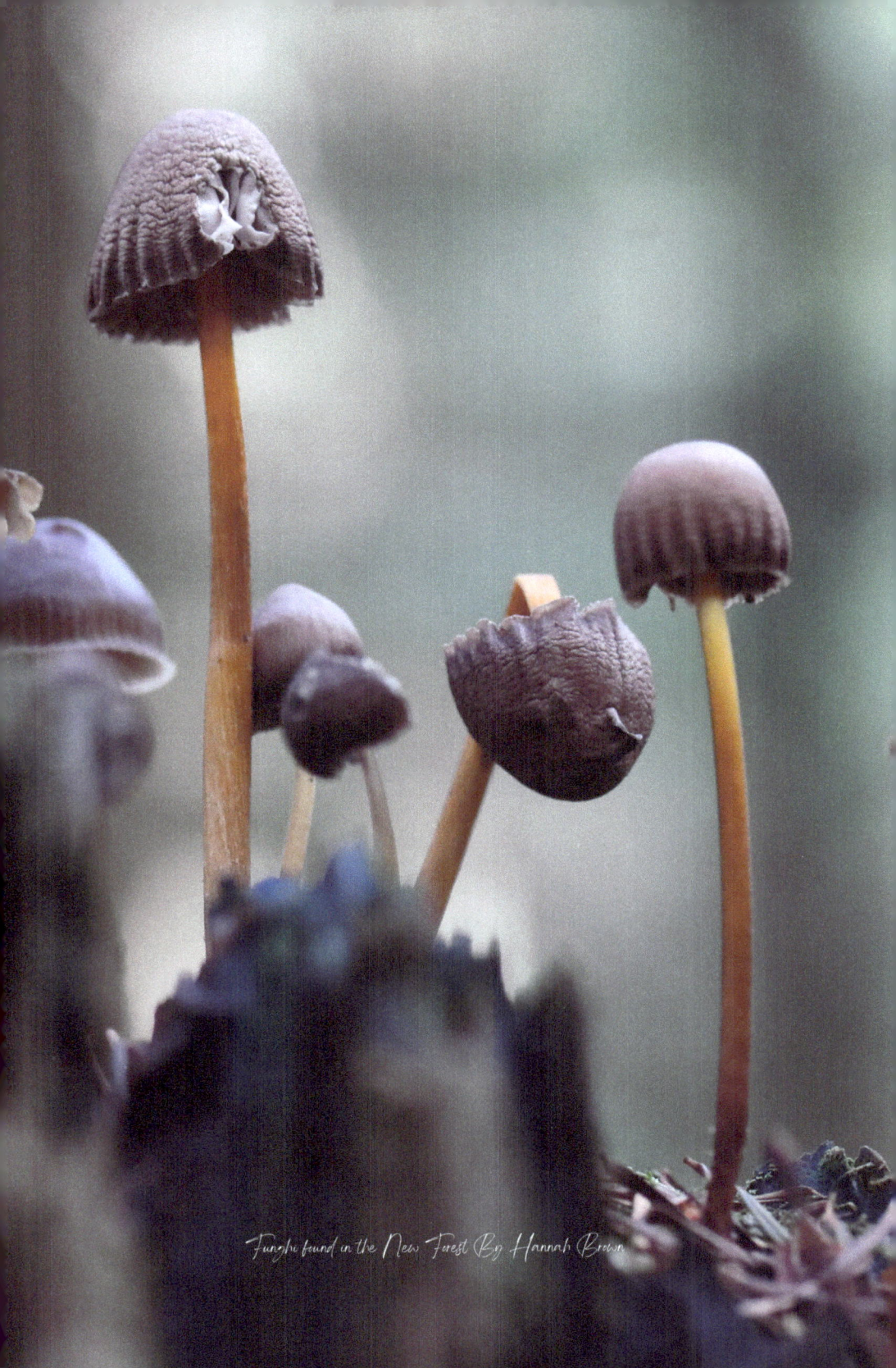
Fungi found in the New Forest By Hannah Brown

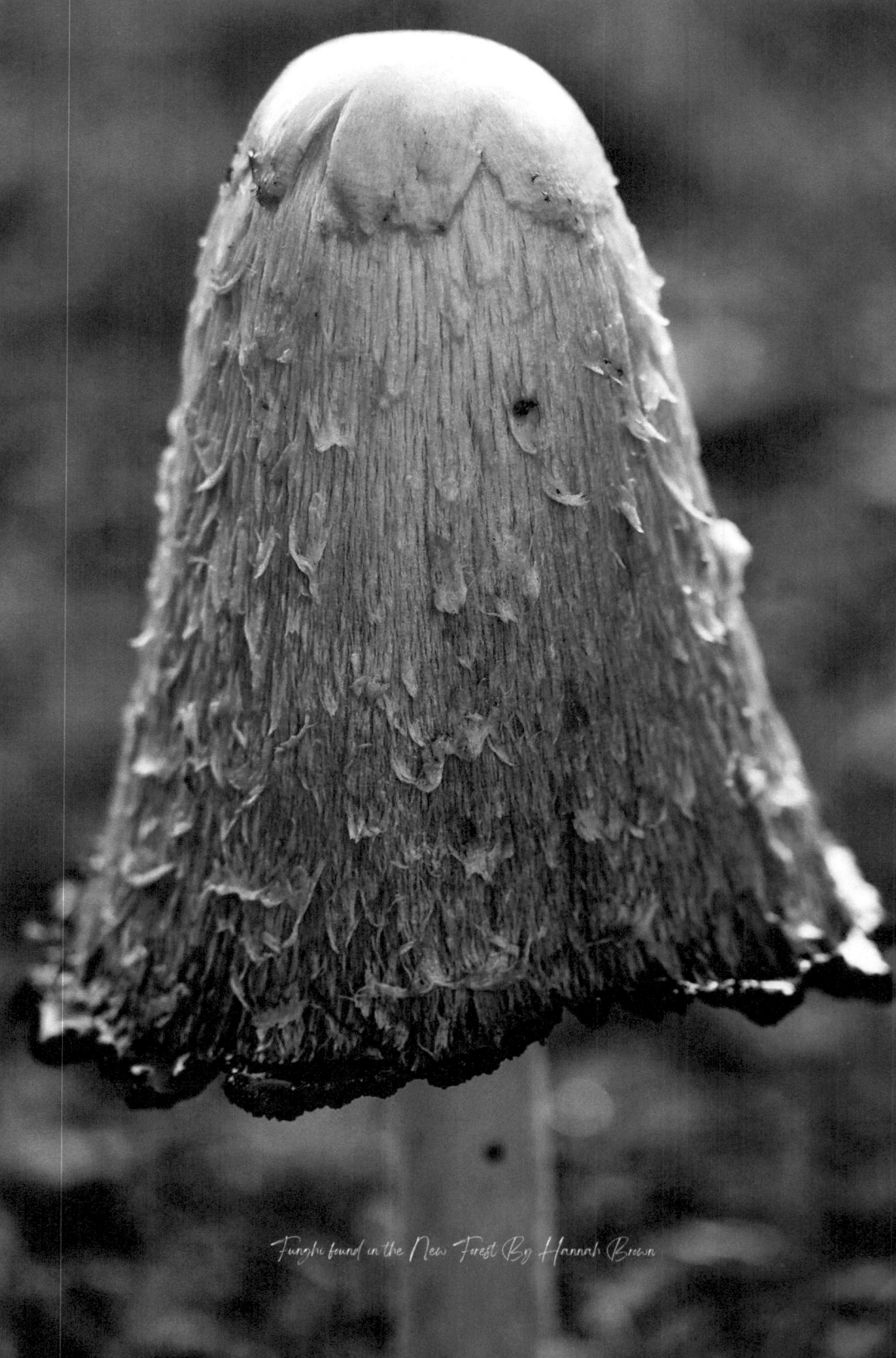

Funghi found in the New Forest By Hannah Brown

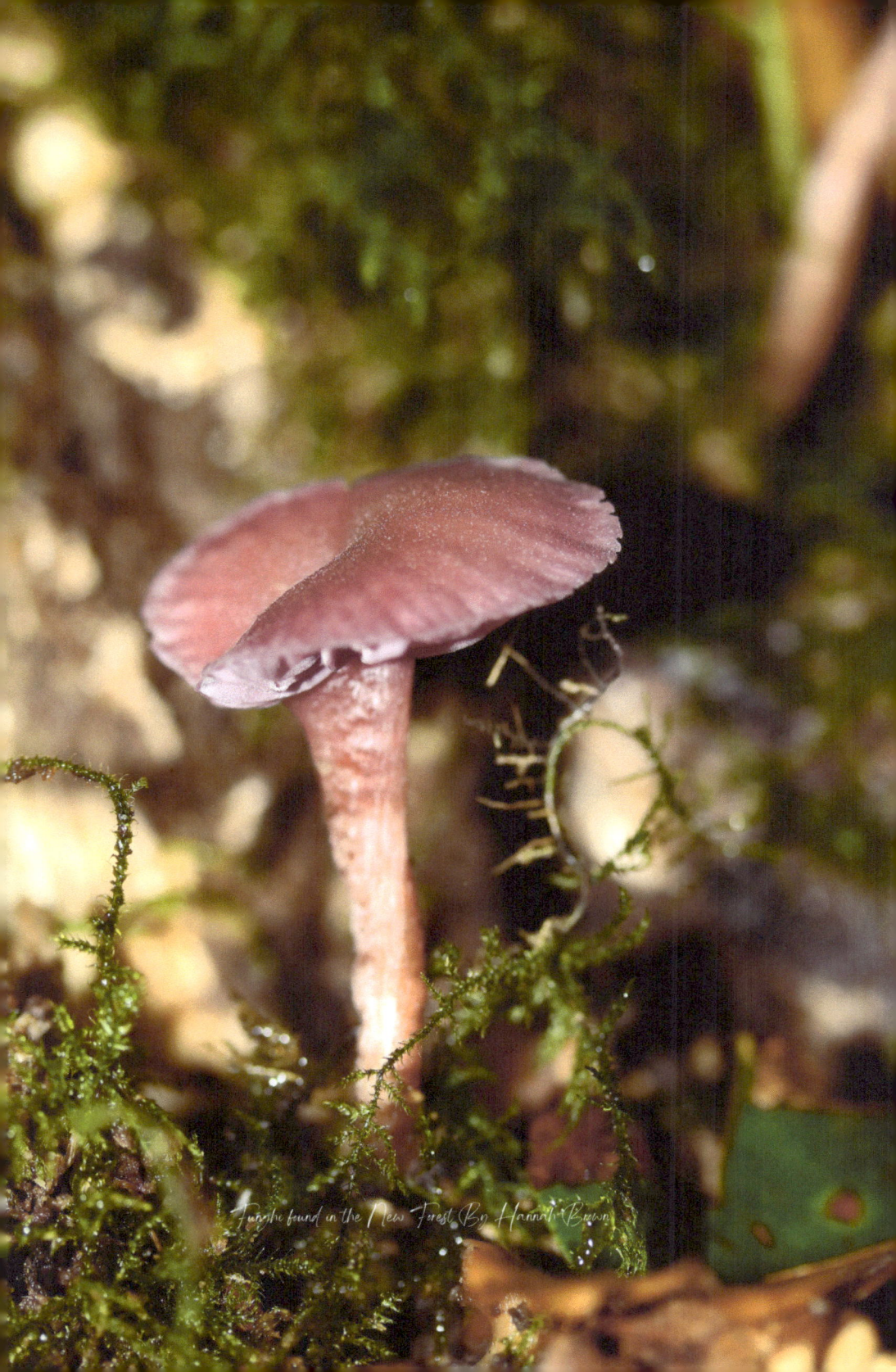
Fungi found in the New Forest By Hannah Brown

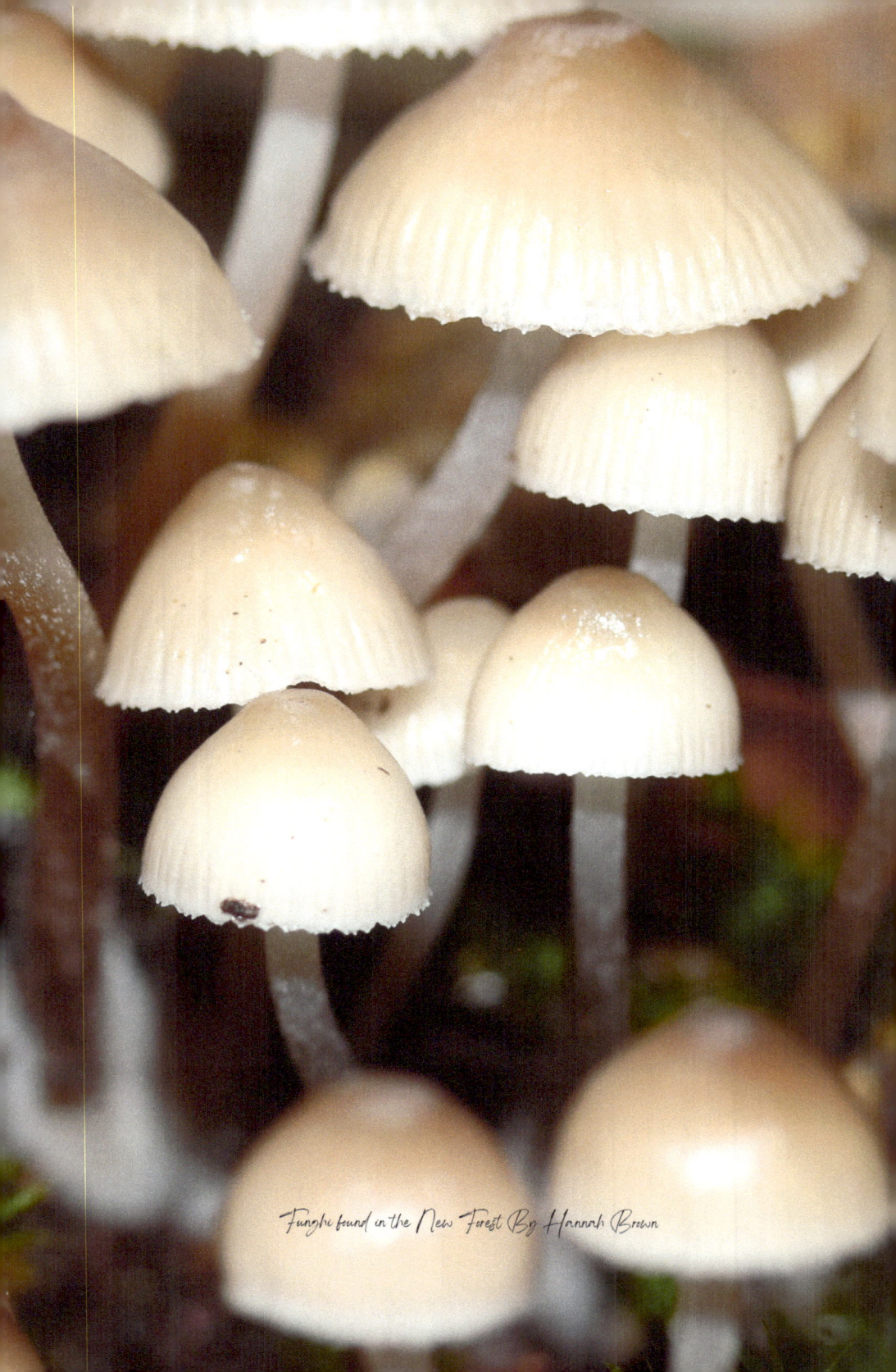

Funghi found in the New Forest By Hannah Brown

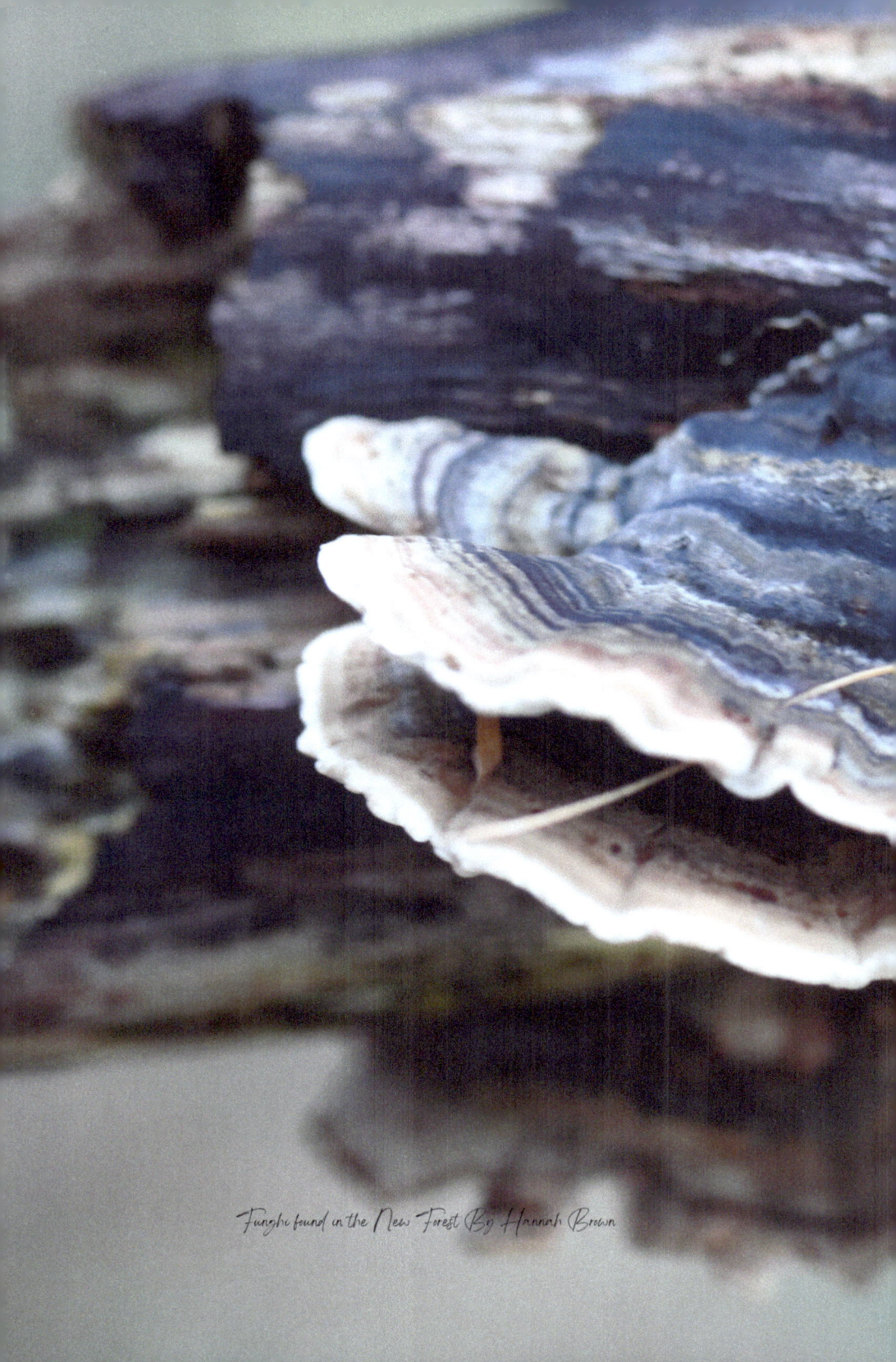

Fungi found in the New Forest By Hannah Brown

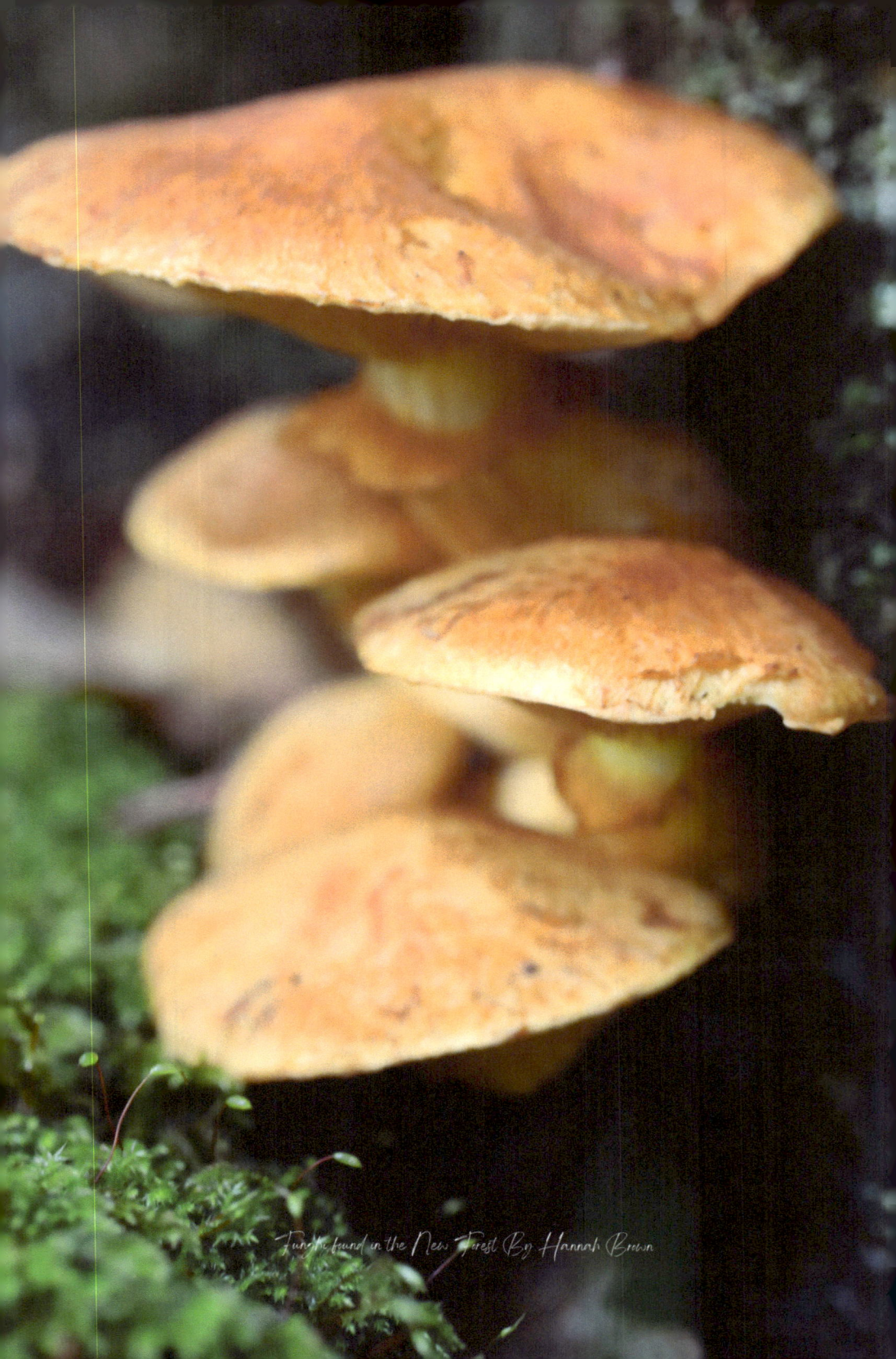

Fungi found in the New Forest By Hannah Brown

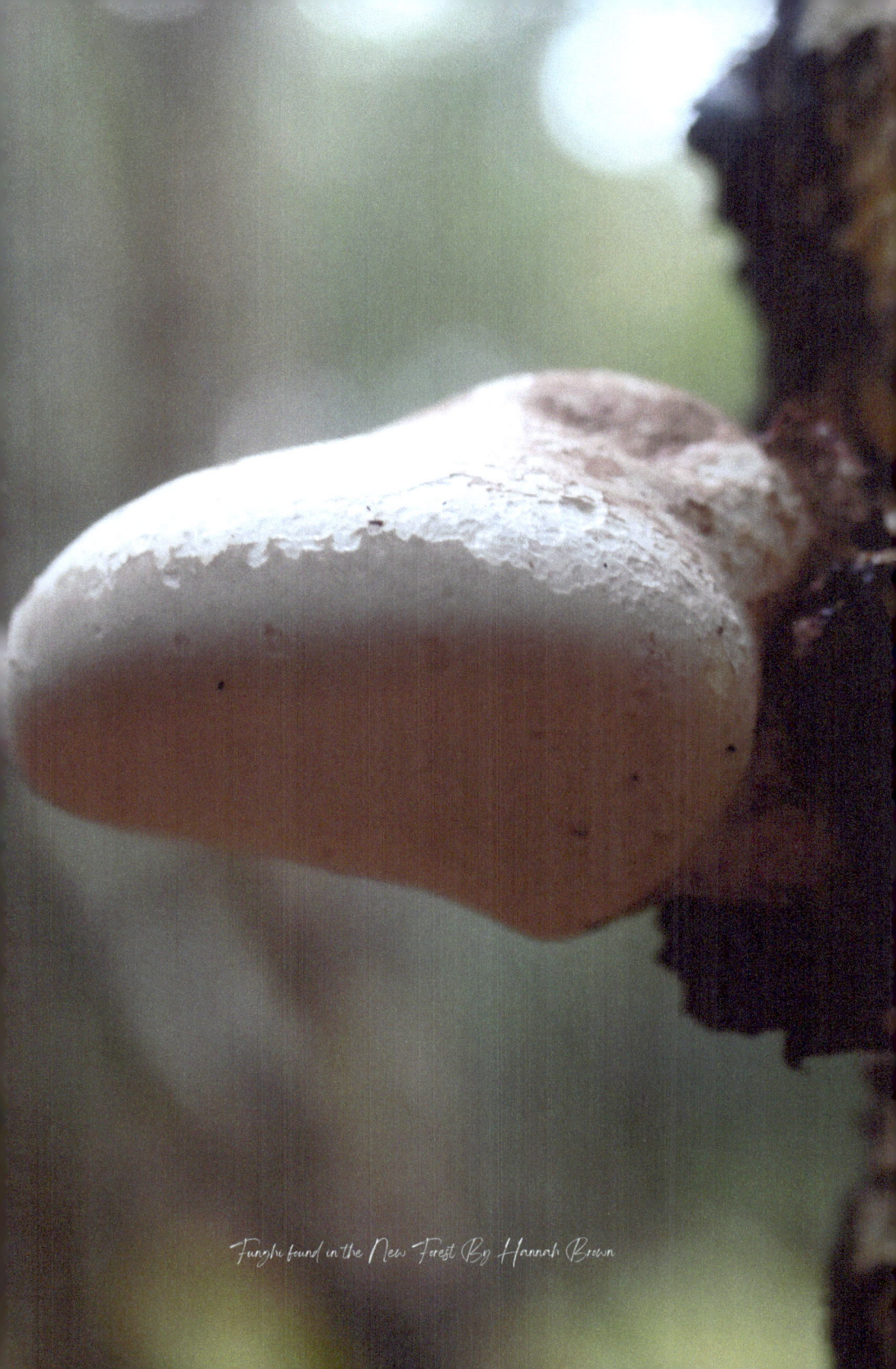

Fungi found in the New Forest By Hannah Brown

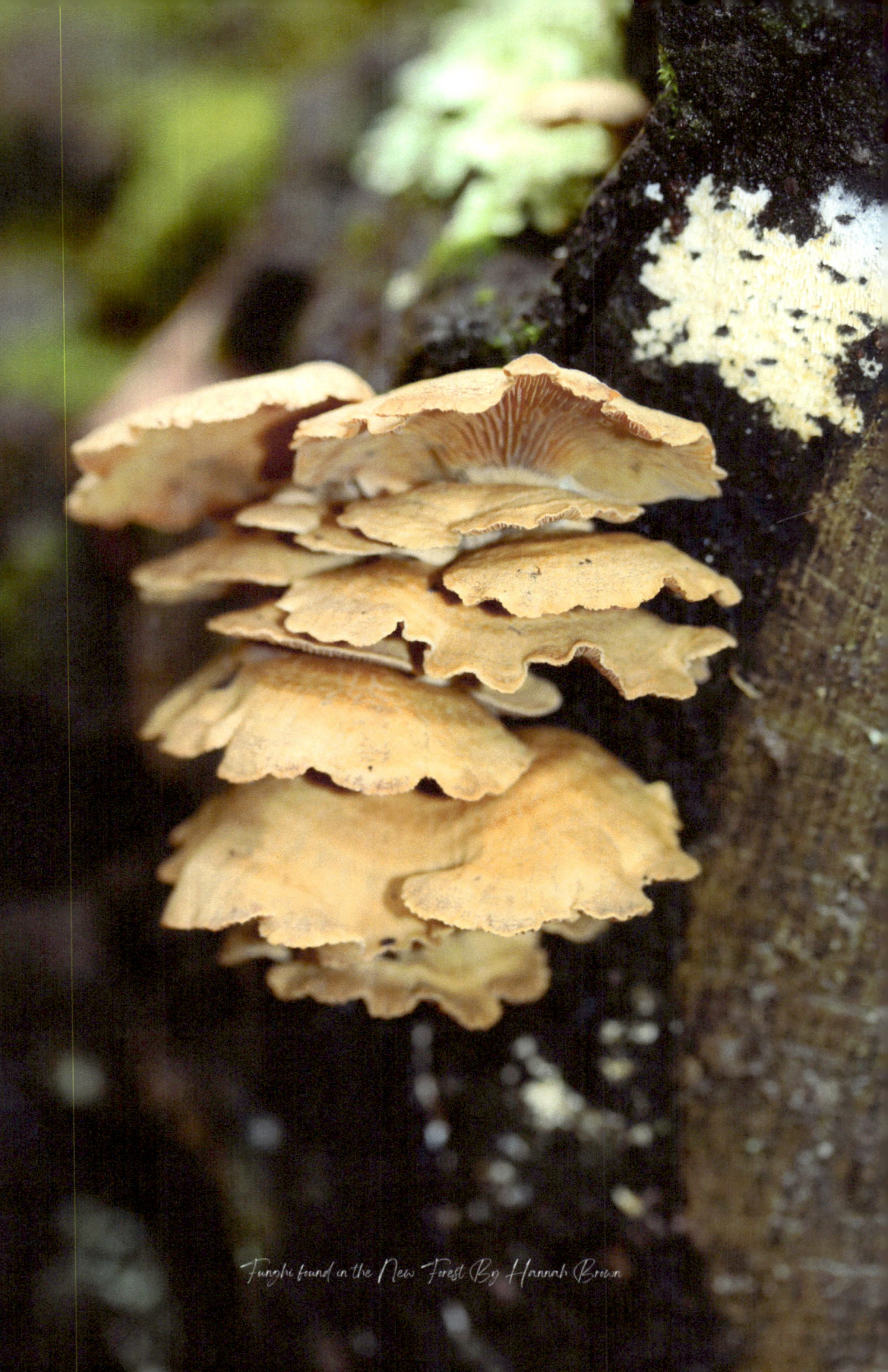

Funghi found in the New Forest By Hannah Brown